RUSSIA
in the twentieth century

NORMAN C. JACKSON B.A.
Senior Lecturer in History, Brentwood College of Education

PERGAMON PRESS

Pergamon Press Ltd., Headington Hill Hall, Oxford, OX3 0BW
Pergamon Press Inc., Maxwell House, Fairview Park, Elmsford, New York 10523
Pergamon of Canada Ltd., PO Box 9600, Don Mills, Ontario M3C 2T9
Pergamon Press (Aust.) Pty Ltd., 19a Boundary Street, Rushcutters Bay, N.S.W. 2011,
Australia

First edition 1975

Printed in Great Britain by A. Wheaton & Co., Exeter

ISBN 0 08 016371 8

RUSSIA IN THE TWENTIETH CENTURY

Contents

Note: Where a word *first* appears in bold type a note can be found in the glossary at the end of the book.

TO JEAN

ACKNOWLEDGEMENTS

The publishers would like to thank the following for permission to reproduce the photographs which appear in this book: the Imperial War Museum, the Novosti Press Agency, the Radio Times Hulton Picture Library and the Society for Cultural Relations with the U.S.S.R.

1 Background to Revolution

THE COUNTRY

A Soviet citizen in Leningrad arrives at work at 9.0 a.m. At the same moment another Soviet citizen, in Anadyr on the east coast, relaxes at home; it is seven o'clock in the evening. This gives some idea of the enormous size of the Soviet Union, which stretches from west to east half way round the world. One half of Europe and one third of Asia are Soviet territory. A journey on the Trans-Siberian railway from Moscow to Vladivostock covers 8800 km and takes eight days. The Soviet Union covers one sixth of the entire land surface of the earth. It is the largest country in the world.

The most northerly of the main natural zones is the treeless *tundra*. The ground is frozen solid for most of the year and reindeer breeding

1

and fur trapping are the main occupations. Below the tundra is the coniferous forest belt, occupying nearly half of the country and providing Russia with the greatest timber resources in the world. The *Steppe* or prairie region further south contains the rich black earth of the Ukraine wheat-belt, as well as much land which is of little agricultural value. Finally there are the deserts of central Asia, mainly unproductive but capable of yielding fine cotton crops when irrigated.

▨	Tundra
⋰	Coniferous forest
⋯	Deciduous forest
▥	Steppe
▤	Semi-desert
▦	Desert

0   500   1000   1500   2000 km

0   500   1000 miles

Map 1 Natural zones in Russia (Today's Frontiers)

Most of Russia is a vast plain over which one may travel for hundreds of miles without seeing a hill over 150 metres high, although one passes many rivers, lakes and marshes. There is an emptiness and wildness about the country which distinguishes it from western Europe. One can journey for mile after mile without seeing a sign of human life. 'Seldom does one see villages . . . they crouch low in the folds of the land as though they wish to be invisible . . .' wrote a German visitor a few years ago. Wolves, which have been extinct in Britain for centuries, still roam forests quite close to Moscow.

The main mountain ranges lie in the south and east of Russia. Mount Elbruz (5547 m) in the Caucasus is the highest peak in Europe. The Caspian Sea is the world's largest expanse of inland water and Lake Baikal is the deepest. Lakes, together with great rivers like the Vishera, Don, Dnieper, Volga and Ob, are important in a country with few good

roads. Russia has all the coal, iron, petroleum and other minerals essential to a modern country.

Most of Russia lies in northerly latitudes far from the sea and there is a much greater difference between summer and winter temperatures than in western Europe. The average July and January temperatures for Moscow are 19°C and −10°C respectively, compared with 18°C and 4°C for London. People wear warm furs and sheepskin boots to keep out the bitter cold of the long winter. Spring comes suddenly in April; the ice of the great rivers breaks up and comes tumbling downstream with deafening crashes. Floods caused by the thaw make transport difficult. The meadows, long covered with snow, are soon carpeted with flowers. All agricultural work has to be crowded into the short season between April and September; then the autumn rains begin and the first snow is not far off.

Fig 1 One of Russia's great rivers, the Vishera in the western Urals.

3

THE PEOPLE

In 1900 the population of Russia was about 130 000 000 and increasing rapidly; it had almost doubled since 1850. Large concentrations of population were found only in parts of European Russia, particularly around the great cities of Moscow and St. Petersburg (now Leningrad). In Siberia there was less than one person per square kilometre. (The average population density for England and Wales is almost 400 people per square kilometre.)

A great variety of people live in Russia, from the blond-haired Slavs of the west to the yellow-skinned Mongols of the east. Over a hundred different languages are used in the country's schools, although Russian is taught everywhere. The majority of Russian people, about 75 per cent, belong to one broad racial group, and are called Slavs. The race originated in western Europe, and Slavs settled in most parts of the country. Thus, similar outlooks and customs are to be found among people right across the vast expanse of Russia, though they may be isolated even from the next village. Customs, like the landscape of the great Russian plain, are changeless.

Peasants

In 1900, over three-quarters of Russia's population were peasants. The typical village consisted of one-roomed log cabins spaced along the edge of a broad unmade track. They were set well apart because of the danger of fire. Inside a hut the walls were blackened by the smoke from the stove and candles illuminated the **icons** (religious pictures) in one corner. The furniture often consisted only of a table and wooden chairs. Many Russian peasants slept on the floor without undressing first, and in the winter they probably slept on top of the large stove which heated their home.

Food was simple and often scarce. The staple diet included coarse black bread and cabbage soup: meat was rarely on the menu. Even the poorest **moujik** (peasant), however, would save for the great feasts which accompanied a marriage or religious festival and which might last several days.

In some areas, these feasts were preceded by a visit to the village bath-house. There, in rooms filled with steam, the peasants sweated violently and beat themselves to stimulate circulation. In winter some of the hardier ones then rushed outside and rolled naked in the snow. Besides cleaning the body, the bath was a fine preparation for the feast since it induced a healthy appetite and an enormous thirst.

During the winter months, when they could not cultivate the land, the peasants worked at home producing anything from lace to harmonicas, according to the speciality of the region. The merchants who bought their products often swindled them by agreeing amongst themselves to pay the craftsmen only the lowest prices for their goods. Some of the more enterprising peasants, in search of better-paid work, migrated to the newly opened lands of Siberia or became factory workers in the towns.

4

Until 1861 the moujiks had been serfs belonging to the Tsar or to local landowners. When an estate passed to a new owner, the serfs went with it. Serfs only retained the right to the land which they farmed in exchange for labour services to the lord, but the moujiks came to regard this land as their own because they had farmed it for so long. The law ending serfdom was issued by Alexander II, the Liberator Tsar; it decreed that the lords should give land to the peasants, who would make a series of repayments for it, lasting over a period of forty-nine years. Many peasants believed that the Tsar had intended them to have the land free, and that the local lord had misunderstood this new law. They expected a further decree written in letters of gold to reveal the true extent of the Tsar's generosity; they waited in vain.

Fig 2 Russian peasants in the late nineteenth century.

5

The moujiks were organized into village groups called **communes,** which were responsible to the Government for their land payments and taxes. The communes divided the land among the peasants. Strips of land in the open fields were allocated to each family, and these were shared out again from time to time to ensure a fair distribution of good and bad soil and to allow for changes in the size of families. The average peasant, using primitive methods of cultivation, had insufficient land and faced starvation when there was a lean harvest. With the rise in population, the size of his landholding grew even smaller. Although free, he was no better off in other respects than when he had been a serf.

The ordinary moujik was religious and superstitious. He had a childish faith in the benevolence of the Tsar, his 'little father' who, he imagined, would come to his aid if only he knew of his plight. Normally the peasant accepted his situation in life with sad resignation in the spirit of the old Russian proverb: 'God is too high and the Tsar is too far away'. At times in the past, however, land-hunger had driven the moujiks into rebellion. In 1900, literacy was slowly spreading and peasant discontent was being encouraged by revolutionaries from the towns. Many moujiks listened with approval when they were told that the estates of the wealthy should really belong to the common people. In some areas barns were pillaged and noblemen's houses burned down, but the police eventually arrived and restored order.

INDUSTRY AND THE WORKERS

Modern factories were not built in Russia until the late nineteenth century. Although her total manufacturing output in 1900 was behind that of the United States of America, Britain, Germany and France, Russia's rate of industrial growth was the fastest in the world. About half of Russia's industry was centred around Moscow, which specialized in cloth, and St. Peterburg, where there were great engineering works. There were important industrial centres in the Ukraine and in Poland, which was then a province of Russia. In the 1890's half of the world's oil was produced at Baku on the Caspian Sea.

By 1900 the total length of the Russian railways was second only to that of the United States of America. Although most of the rail system was in Europe, work was well advanced on the great Trans-Siberian line to link Moscow to Vladivostok on the Pacific coast. Sixty per cent of the railways were Government-owned and the State played an important part in the general development of industry. The Tsar raised a lot of his revenue by controlling the production and sale of alcohol. Foreign capital flowed into Russia and was particularly important in developing the oil and coal industries.

Russia's late development as an industrial nation allowed her to miss the early stages of the factory system; she was able to begin with large-scale production in many factories. In 1900, three quarters of Russia's factory workers were employed in big firms with a labour force of more than a thousand. Not even the United States of America had such a high proportion of large factories.

Russia, however, was not spared the social evils of the industrial revolution: child labour, unhealthy working conditions, long hours, low pay and insanitary housing. It is true that by 1900 the working day was by law limited to eleven and a half hours and that it was illegal to employ children under the age of fifteen; however, there were few factory inspectors and these regulations were often evaded. The average wage for an adult worker in Moscow was fifteen roubles (£1.50) a month; in London he would have earned about three times as much.

Half of the workmen lived in hostels attached to the factories, where accommodation was either free or very cheap. Here many families shared one large room divided up by cloth hangings or wooden partitions. Sometimes the same beds were occupied continuously by alternate night and day shifts. The factory hostels often looked and smelled like overcrowded stables. Still worse off were the workers in some small woollen mills. The family lived where they worked, sleeping on boards above the looms at night with the baby perhaps in a cradle hooked to the ceiling.

However, the picture was not one of complete gloom. A few employers, mainly owners of large-scale enterprises, built decent homes for their workers and even provided schools and hospitals.

The peasant-turned-industrial-worker would often find it too expensive to maintain his wife and children in the village. He would send for them to add to the family income and to share his wretched existence. In 1900, some 20 per cent of the Russian population lived in the towns, which were growing rapidly as people flocked in from the countryside. The population of Moscow had tripled in thirty years.

The concentration of workers in large factories provided ideal conditions for the growth of trade unions, but these were illegal. Strikers could be accused of plotting a revolt and could be forced back to work at the point of a bayonet. The herding together of the workers in miserable conditions also presented a fruitful field of activity for Communist revolutionaries, who preached the overthrow of the factory owners and the Tsarist government which supported them. The workers were then to be the ones to elect the government and control the factories.

THE TSAR AND GOVERNMENT

Tsar Peter the Great, in the late seventeenth century, began to force western ideas down the throats of his reluctant subjects. He made his courtiers wear European clothes and appear clean-shaven: if he met a bearded nobleman in the street, he would grab him by the beard and cut it off there and then. To modernize life in as vast a country as Russia required an able and determined ruler. Tsar Nicholas II, who reigned in 1900, was no such person.

As a boy, Nicholas had been present at the bloody deathbed of his grandfather, Alexander II, whose reforms had not saved him from a terrorist's bomb. Nicholas's father, Alexander III, a huge bearded man who could tie pokers in knots, had the physical strength of Tsar Peter but not his lively brain. He concluded that reforms were dangerous and gave up no shred of his authority despite attempts to assassinate him.

When Nicholas II became Tsar in 1894 he was only twenty-six years old. In character he was shy, kindly and weak-willed. After his marriage in 1895 he was much influenced by his German-born wife. Slim and handsome, the young Tsar much resembled his cousin, the future George V of England. His outlook, however, corresponded very closely to that of Charles I, an English King of 250 years earlier. Charles' attempt to keep absolute personal control over the country had led him to the scaffold. A similar fate awaited Nicholas.

During the coronation ceremonies in Moscow, a great crowd gathered for the traditional presentation of small gifts. A rumour spread that

Fig 3 Tsar Nicholas II standing with his son Alexis (the Tsarevitch), his second daughter Grand Duchess Tatiana, and Prince Nikita.

there were not enough to go round, and in the subsequent scramble hundreds were trampled to death. Those people who saw in this an ill omen for the reign were not mistaken.

Entries in Nicholas's diary such as 'Walked long and killed two crows' reveal a fondness for physical activity which was not matched by an interest in political affairs. The Tsar had little understanding of the great effect that industrial changes were having on Russian society. 'I shall maintain the principle of absolute power just as firmly and unswervingly as did my late and unforgettable father', he wrote in 1895. Nicholas displayed a considerable talent for choosing corrupt, inefficient or even mad ministers. He had not the common sense to back up the few able men who came into his service.

Below the Tsar and his chosen ministers was a huge number of officials who carried out their orders. These civil servants were carefully graded in a 'table of ranks' which not only decided their pay but also their place in society and the title by which they were addressed. A school inspector was entitled to be called 'Excellency'.

The most sinister and corrupt of the State servants were the secret police. It was their job to seek out revolutionaries, but they oppressed all who voiced opposition to the Government. Criticism was regarded as disloyalty; newspapers and books were scrupulously censored. People arrested for anti-government activity were imprisoned or sent to the wastelands of Siberia. Minority races like the Lithuanians, Georgians and Jews were closely supervised. Any attempts to form movements which might prove disloyal to the Tsar were put down. Some of the secret police took a special delight in encouraging **pogroms** (organized assaults) upon the large Jewish population: hundreds were killed in these cruel massacres. Blaming Jews for the poverty of Russia turned criticism away from the government.

In Britain, by the late nineteenth century working-class men were able to take part in the election of the government which ruled them. This was not the case in Russia. Elected representatives played no part in the Central Government, which was headed by the Tsar. The **zemstva** (county councils), which were established by Alexander II, had elected members. Peasants could vote in the zemstva elections but the system was arranged to favour the nobility. The zemstva were responsible for schools, hospitals, roads and poor relief in their areas. Although subject to increasing interference by the Central Government they did useful work, especially in the development of education. There were also town councils elected by the wealthy residents. The Tsar described as 'senseless dreams' the demands made by some zemstva for elected members in the Central Government. A number of zemstva leaders formed an illegal party, the 'Union of Liberation', to further their aims.

The Government persecuted those who openly criticized it and thus forced opposition underground, where it rankled, grew and developed into violent and revolutionary movements. Among the revolutionaries was a small but dedicated group who fought the might of the Tsar's empire with the ideas of a German writer, Karl Marx.

SUMMARY – Chapter 1

THE COUNTRY
Russia, the world's largest country, covers one sixth of the land surface
of the globe. The main natural zones are the tundra, coniferous forest
belt, steppes and deserts of central Asia. Most of Russia is a vast plain
with great lakes and rivers. Russia contains all the minerals needed for
industry. Much of the country lies in northerly inland regions having
short summers and long cold winters.

POPULATION
Russia's population in 1900 was 130 million and increasing rapidly.
There were only large concentrations of population in European Russia.
There were many races in the country but most people were Slavs.

PEASANTS
In 1900 three-quarters of Russia's people were poor peasants (moujiks)
using primitive farming methods. Village organizations called
communes arranged the raising of taxes and sharing out of the land.
Until 1861 the moujiks were serfs. They were discontented, and some
supported revolutionaries.

INDUSTRY AND THE WORKERS
Russian industries were behind those of the advanced Western
countries in 1900 but were growing rapidly. Moscow and St. Petersburg
were large industrial centres. The Government played a large part in
developing railways. About 20 per cent of Russia's people lived in
towns. Factory workers, including children, worked long hours in poor
conditions for low wages. Communists worked among them for the
overthrow of the factory owners and the Tsar.

THE TSAR AND GOVERNMENT
Tsar Nicholas II believed he alone had the right to rule Russia. He had
little interest in politics and was unwise in his choice of ministers.
There were no elected members in the Tsar's government although the
county councils (zemstva) and town councils had elected members.
Revolutionary movements were kept down by the secret police, who
also persecuted minority races.

2 Lenin and the Russian Revolutions

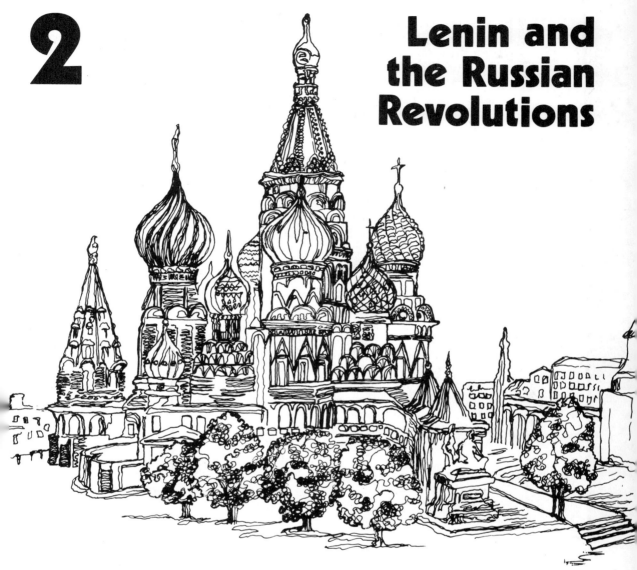

KARL MARX AND COMMUNISM

'Let the governing classes tremble before the Communist revolution. The workers have nothing to lose in it but their chains. Workers of the world, unite!' These stirring words appeared in the *Communist Manifesto* in 1848. Their author was Karl Marx, a German who had escaped from his native country after taking part in a rebellion. Marx spent nearly all the rest of his life in England, often working in the Reading Room of the British Museum. His political ideas were set out in a huge book called *Das Kapital*. They form the basis of the political belief known as **Communism.**

Marx wrote at a time when mechanical inventions, especially the steam engine, were bringing important changes to the industries of western Europe. Factories were springing up and in them the workers, children as well as adults, often worked long hours in miserable conditions. The poor pay allowed the factory-workers to rent only crowded and insanitary homes. Marx believed that this situation, in which the workers were exploited by their employers, would get worse and worse until finally the workers would rebel. This would bring to an end the system known as **Capitalism,** in which a small class of property owners (the Capitalists) became wealthy through the efforts of the working class. Then the working class would form the government, removing all power from the former ruling classes. Later, after a series of workers' revolutions all round the world, the true Communist society would be able to develop. In this the principle of 'from each according to his ability, to each according to his need' would be followed: people would work willingly for the common good at the occupation for which they were most suited, and in return they would receive without charge, the food, clothes, housing and services which they needed.

LENIN'S EARLY LIFE

In Russia at the turn of the century one of the most able and inspired Communists was a young man called Vladimir Ulyanov, better known as Lenin. He was born in 1870 at the town of Simbirsk on the Volga; it is now called Ulyanovsk in his honour. Lenin's father was an education officer who was often away visiting the widely scattered schools of his area. Lenin inherited his father's red hair and, more important, his energy and intelligence. Young Vladimir was first educated at home. When he went to the local high school he made rapid progress.

On 13 March 1887 six students, three of them clutching fat books, stood waiting at the side of a road along which the Tsar was to pass. The books contained home-made bombs. Police discovered this before the Tsar's arrival and among those arrested was Alexander Ulyanov, Lenin's older brother. Alexander could have saved his life by expressing regret for his action; he refused to do so. 'I didn't want to escape. I wished to die for my country', he told the court. Up to this time Lenin had shown no interest in politics, but he was deeply affected by his brother's execution. Shortly afterwards Lenin was sent down from the university where he had begun to study law for taking part in a student demonstration. (Although he was not allowed to return to the university, he did qualify as a lawyer.) It was the first step along the road which he was to follow until his death. For this offence, Lenin spent a short time in jail. 'My path has been blazed by my older brother', he told a fellow prisoner. It was from Alexander's copy of Marx's *Das Kapital* that Lenin learned the revolutionary ideas which were to change the face of Russia.

In 1895 Lenin went abroad to meet exiled Communists. On his return, he smuggled in revolutionary literature in a trunk with a false bottom. The secret police were soon on his trail; he was arrested and imprisoned. Lenin quickly settled down to prison routine and invented

Fig 4 Vladimir
Ulyanov (Lenin)
as a schoolboy.

a knock code to play chess with a man in a neighbouring cell. He began writing, and said rather regretfully on his release, 'If I had been in prison longer I could have finished the book'.

After his year's imprisonment, Lenin was sent into exile into Siberia. He had to arrange the journey himself and to travel at his own expense. Eventually he arrived at the village of Shushenkoye after travelling on the Trans-Siberian railway and crossing the River Ob on horseback. In exile Lenin was certainly not persecuted by the police; he bought a dog and went out shooting ducks, and in the winter he enjoyed ice-skating on the frozen river. His fiancée Nadya, a fellow Communist was also exiled and allowed to join him in Siberia. They were married there in 1898. Lenin carried on with his writing and corresponded with his Communist friends, some of whom even came to visit him.

Soon after his exile ended in 1900, Lenin went abroad, Nadya following him when her sentence was completed. The Ulyanovs travelled around Europe, living for periods in Munich, Paris and London. In London, Lenin, like Karl Marx before him, found the British Museum useful for writing and study. Nadya shocked their landlady because she did not wear a wedding ring or put up curtains. It was in London that Lenin first met Lev Bronstein, a young Jewish Russian. Bronstein had spent some time in Russian prisons and now called himself Trotsky, which had been the name of one of his warders. He and Lenin could hardly have realized how important their partnership was later to become.

While abroad Lenin wrote for a revolutionary newspaper called *Iskra (The Spark)*, which was smuggled back into Russia and distributed among workers and peasants. The first issue was seized by the police, but later editions were smuggled in by sailors or dropped overboard in waterproof bundles to be picked up later by Communist agents.

In 1903 a number of Russian revolutionaries, members of the **Social Democratic Party** formed in 1898, met in a warehouse in Brussels. When the Belgian police refused to let them hold their meetings, the whole conference moved on to London. It split into two parts: the **Bolsheviks** (majority group), led by Lenin, believed that the party should be closely controlled by a small group of leaders who would work full-time for revolution in Russia; the **Mensheviks** (minority group) believed in a loosely organized party which would work with other groups to bring about a change of Government in Russia. Lenin, as usual, had little time for those who would not accept his ideas and violently attacked the Mensheviks. His impatience and scorn cost him influence and friends; Trotsky turned away from him at this time. Yet nothing diverted Lenin from planning the overthrow of the Government. 'He even talked revolution in his sleep', Nadya wrote.

WAR BETWEEN RUSSIA AND JAPAN (1904-1905)

At the turn of the century the Chinese empire was disintegrating and Russia and Japan were both anxious to occupy Chinese lands. When the Russians managed to persuade the Chinese to allow them to build the Trans-Siberian railway across Manchuria, the Japanese were understandably annoyed. Russia had troops in Manchuria which she had agreed to withdraw, but she failed to do so.

The Tsar's advisers realized how angry the Japanese were but most of them did not worry. 'A short victorious war . . . would stem the tide of revolution', said one of the ministers. War might turn the people's minds away from the miserable conditions at home; it might end the peasant risings in the countryside and the factory workers' strikes in the towns.

The Russians, with the permission of the Chinese, controlled Port Arthur and stationed some of their Pacific fleet there. The Japanese attacked Port Arthur without warning in February 1904, and in a few months Japan had gained complete control of the Pacific. The Russians now made a desperate move. They ordered their Baltic fleet, which was hopelessly slow and out of date, to sail almost round the world to attack the Japanese in the Pacific. Early in the voyage, the Russian crews nervously opened fire on British trawlers, which they mistook for Japanese torpedo boats. For a while the incident seemed likely to bring Britain into the war but the Tsar's apologies and generous compensation settled the matter. On 27 May 1905, after an eight months' voyage, the Russian ships met the enemy fleet off the island of Tsushima (between Japan and Korea). In a few hours the Russians

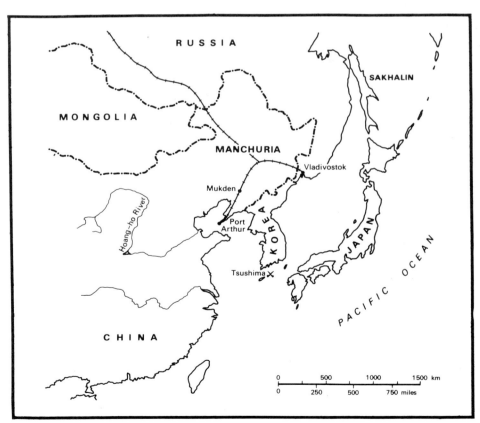

Map 2 The Russo-Japanese War 1904-1905

15

suffered a staggering defeat. Twenty-two of their ships were sunk and others were captured. Thousands of sailors drowned. Only three small vessels reached safety in Vladivostok. The modern Japanese fleet, commanded skilfully by Admiral Togo, had shown its superiority.

On land the Russians fared no better. Their overland supply system to Manchuria was poor and the Japanese controlled the sea. Defeat followed defeat. Port Arthur fell, and in March 1905 a Russian army was beaten at Mukden in Manchuria.

The Tsar's government had stumbled into a war which it was quite incapable of winning. Encouraged by the U.S.A., which acted as a peace-maker, Japan and Russia signed a peace treaty in August 1905. Russia gave up Port Arthur and part of the island of Sakhalin (see the map on the previous page).

The Tsar's losses of territory were not important. Far more serious was his loss of the Russian people's confidence.

The 1905 revolution

In 1905 a handsome young priest, George Gapon, was working as a police agent in St. Petersburg. His task was to organize a trade union among the factory workers. This operated peacefully and kept the leadership of the workers out of the hands of dangerous revolutionaries. However, the workers were becoming restless. A sharp rise in the cost of living had bitten deeply into their low wages. Disgust at Russia's defeats in the Japanese war spurred them to action. Many of these trade unionists still regarded the Tsar as their true protector; they blamed Russia's failures on his ministers. The workers decided to present a petition to the Tsar asking for an end to the war, an elected Parliament, an eight-hour day and increased wages. This petition was written in the most humble terms: 'We, the workers of the city of St. Petersburg, our wives, children and helpless old parents are approaching Thee, our Lord, to seek justice and protection. We live in misery, we are oppressed, we are burdened with work beyond our strength.'

Father Gapon was not keen on the petition but he was now the prisoner of events. On a cold Sunday morning in late January 1905, he walked at the head of a procession of about 150 000 people. As the crowd approached the Winter Palace through the snow-covered streets they saw that troops were drawn up in front of the building. The demonstrators carried icons and portraits of the Tsar. They called on Nicholas to come out to meet them, unaware that he had left St. Petersburg for his nearby country estate. As the crowd surged forward, shots rang out and the white snow became stained with blood. When the people had dispersed under the hail of bullets about six hundred lay dead in the square. Father Gapon was horrified by the massacre. 'Rivers of blood separate the Tsar from the people. Long live freedom!' he declared. Gapon afterwards fled abroad and joined the Social Revolutionaries, a party which drew its support mainly from the peasants. His comrades later suspected that he had renewed his contacts with the Russian secret police; in April 1906 they lured him to an isolated cottage in Finland and hanged him as a traitor.

16

Fig 5 George
Gapon, priest and
Labour leader.

17

As the news of 'Bloody Sunday' spread, revolts broke out all over the country and continued throughout 1905. The Tsar's uncle fell victim to a terrorist bomb. Factory workers downed tools and even ballet dancers came out on strike. The peasants, usually slow to take action, turned to violence. In many parts of Russia they burned the landowners' mansions and carried off the grain from their barns. About 2000 estates were despoiled in this way. The secret police followed their usual tactics of turning the anger of the people away from the Government towards the Jews, by blaming them for Russia's troubles. Many Jews suffered in pogroms, but ill-feeling towards the Tsar's government did not lessen. Even the troops called out to deal with these riots could not always be trusted. The cruelty and inefficiency of the government was beginning to destroy the loyalty of the armed forces.

In June there was a dramatic naval mutiny. The sailors of the battleship Potemkin seized control from their officers. For some days they sailed menacingly through the Black Sea but they did not know how to follow up their success, and eventually they entered a Romanian port and gave themselves up. Twenty years later this incident was made into a magnificent film by Sergei Eisenstein.

The uprisings of 1905 surprised the Social Democrats and they were slow to take advantage of them. In the spring Trotsky smuggled himself back into Russia but the attentions of the secret police forced him into hiding. When a new wave of strikes broke out in the autumn, Trotsky helped to set up a workers' council **(soviet)** in St. Petersburg. The factory workers elected representatives to the council, which organized strikes and demonstrations. Although this workers' council lasted only a few weeks, it set an important pattern for the future.

Tsar Nicholas had not intended the massacre of Bloody Sunday: it had been a horrible mistake. Afterwards he expressed his sorrow to a carefully chosen group of workers and contributed to a fund for the families of those killed by his soldiers. The revolution of 1905 brought to a head the widespread demand that Nicholas should reform his government; he bowed reluctantly before the storm and issued the *October Manifesto*. This declared that all Russians had the right to freedom of speech and of religion. It also promised, for the first time in Russian history, an elected Parliament, the **Duma.** Although all classes were to take part in elections for the Duma, the voting system favoured the rich. The Tsar could still appoint the ministers of his government and he would control the armed forces. Laws would need the approval of the Tsar and the Duma, but the Tsar could pass them alone when the Duma was not sitting.

Confirmed revolutionaries like Lenin proclaimed that the October Manifesto was a fraud. Nothing would satisfy them but that the Tsar and his government should be completely swept away. The Socialist parties (Social Democrats and **Social Revolutionary Party**) refused to take part in elections to the Duma. Others, less extreme in their views, were willing to give the Duma a chance.

By December 1905 the revolution, like the year itself, was drawing to a close. The most dramatic of the final scenes took place in Moscow where the army had to use cannon to smash the barricades set up by workers. As the last embers of revolt died away the way was clear for a new start in Russia. People eagerly awaited the first meeting of the Duma.

Stolypin and the Duma

The Duma first met in early May 1906 in the Throne Room of the Winter Palace. To one side stood the Tsar in his magnificent uniform of white, surrounded by his courtiers; on the other side of the room were the newly elected members, some 450 of them. Over half were workers from farm or industry, and many were wearing their everyday clothes — peasants' blouses or factory overalls. The atmosphere was strange and tense. Stolypin, one of Nicholas's ministers, gazed round uneasily in the fear that someone might be concealing a bomb.

When the speeches began, member after member rose to call on the Tsar to dismiss his ministers. They demanded the right to strike, the sharing out of the nobles' estates among the peasants and the freeing of political prisoners. But the gap between the Tsar and the Duma was too great to bridge. When the representatives arrived at the palace for the next meeting on 22 July, they found their way barred by soldiers. The first Duma had come to an end.

The Socialist parties took part in the elections to the second Duma; consequently this body was even more hostile to the Tsar than the first and was dismissed in 1907. Then, without consulting the Duma, Nicholas altered the election system so that the working class for the most part lost their votes. The next Duma, elected in 1907, consisted mainly of representatives of the wealthy classes. As might be expected, it was more friendly towards the Tsar, and it was allowed to run its full five years in office.

During this period the Tsar had one outstanding servant, Peter Stolypin, who became Prime Minister in 1906. Stolypin's actions against revolutionaries in 1905 marked him as a tough and ruthless character. One of his first moves on gaining power was to set up committees to arrest people suspected of disloyalty. Nevertheless, Stolypin could see better than most that imprisoning revolutionaries would not by itself prevent a revolution. The Government needed the support of the people if it was to remain in power. Stolypin believed that the peasants would provide this if agriculture could be made prosperous. In co-operation with the Duma, he carried through a series of important reforms.

In 1906 peasants were relieved of the heavy payments for their land which they had made since serfdom ended in 1861. A peasant was allowed to possess his own land instead of it belonging to the village group (the commune). His scattered strips of land in the open fields could now be brought together into one farm.

Many peasants took a pride in personally owning their land. They worked hard and began to use modern farming methods. By 1909 over a million peasant families had their own farms. In areas where there was a land shortage, peasants were given Government help to go as pioneer farmers to the vast empty plains of Siberia. Three and a half million people moved under this scheme in ten years.

Farming certainly became more efficient but Stolypin's plans needed much time: 'twenty years of quiet', as he put it. Many peasants who had not enough land to live on sold what they had and became farm labourers. These men were often jealous of the wealthier land-owning peasants (**kulaks**) and they were likely to listen to revolutionary ideas. Moreover, the rural population was growing fast, making it harder to raise the standard of living. Thus Stolypin's attempt to bring contentment to the countryside benefited only a minority of the peasants.

During Stolypin's time industry, too, was taking fast strides. Output of coal and iron doubled between 1905 and 1913. Railways expanded quickly and many more factories were built. Although life was still hard for the industrial worker, his pay and conditions gradually improved.

Stolypin also started to develop Russia's education system. In 1908 he began a campaign through the zemstva to stamp out illiteracy. There was a great increase in school building and in five years the expenditure on schools doubled.

In all these ways Russia made progress under Stolypin's guidance, but it was only a start. In industry, agriculture, and education, Russia was still well behind countries like Germany and Britain.

Stolypin's career ended dramatically in 1911. One night in St. Petersburg he was attending an opera at which the Tsar was also present. Nicholas later wrote that he had just left the royal box when 'I heard two sounds as if something had been dropped. I thought that an opera glass might have been dropped on someone's head.' Women began to scream and it was obvious that something much more serious had occurred. Nicholas then saw Stolypin standing opposite the royal box. At first he only noticed how pale he was. Then Nicholas saw that Stolypin was clutching his chest where his uniform was stained with blood. Stolypin made the sign of the cross and collapsed. The Tsar's most talented minister had fallen victim to a revolutionary's bullets.

THE FIRST WORLD WAR AND THE MARCH REVOLUTION

After her defeat by Japan, Russia gave up any thoughts of extending eastwards. Instead she turned her attention westwards and southwards, towards eastern Europe and Turkey. This was an area in which Austria, then the centre of a large empire, was also interested. Russia already had a treaty of friendship with France, and now she strengthened her position by coming to terms with an old enemy, Britain, to settle disputes over India and Persia.

On 28 June 1914, Archduke Ferdinand, heir to the Austrian throne, was murdered by Serbians. Serbia was a small East European state whose people were Slavs, the same race as the majority of Russians. Although the Serbian government did all it could to make amends, nothing would stop the Austrians from declaring war. Russia was

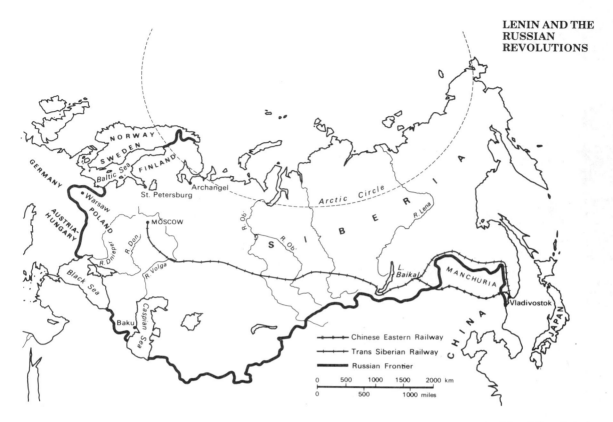

Map 3 Russia in 1914

bound to support Serbia. Germany backed up Austria. Soon France and Britain, Russia's allies, were involved in the war too.

A great crowd assembled before the Tsar's palace when war was declared and Nicholas made a brave speech which was wildly cheered. Russia started the war united and full of hope. Grand Duke Nicholas, the Tsar's uncle, was made commander in chief of the army and millions of young men flocked to the colours.

The Grand Duke had planned to hold the Germans in the north while he attacked the weaker Austrian army in the south, but the Russians were persuaded by the French to attack the Germans too. The idea was to force Germany to divert soldiers from the armies moving into France.

In the south, the Russians pushed the Austrian army back. They took hundreds of thousands of prisoners, although at heavy cost to themselves. To the north it was a different story. The advance into German Prussia was halted at Tannenberg and the Russian troops were sent reeling back. The German army was superior in leadership, weapons and training. Russian generals often owed their positions more to their noble birth than to any military skill they might have possessed. Supplies, particularly of weapons and ammunition, were short; by August 1915 one third of the Russian soldiers were without rifles. They marched into battle unarmed until they could snatch a weapon from the hand of a fallen comrade.

21

Fig 6 1914-18 war. A Russian battery in action.

Germany decided to smash Russia before dealing with France. Two-thirds of the German army were sent to fight on the Russian front. In this way, Russia was saving France, but she was bleeding to death in the effort. In one year of fighting she suffered 4 million casualties. At this time of disaster Tsar Nicholas felt that it was his duty to take command of the army. After Nicholas left Petrograd for the front, the real ruler of Russia was his wife, the Tsarina Alexandra. Alexandra was unpopular because of her German birth and because she was in the habit of taking advice from a man called Gregory Rasputin.

Rasputin was such a fantastic character that it is difficult to separate the tales invented about him from the truth. He wore long robes and called himself a monk. Although often unwashed and carelessly dressed, his striking appearance and personality won him the favours of many women. Among these were titled ladies who introduced him into Court, where the Tsarina herself fell under Rasputin's spell. It happened that Alexandra's only son, the heir to the throne, suffered from the incurable blood disease known as **haemophilia.** It soon appeared that the presence of Rasputin could improve the boy's condition. Indeed, Rasputin could apparently achieve this effect even from a distance, by speaking over the telephone. The Tsar and his wife came to believe that Rasputin had been sent by God to look after their family and the Russian people.

Fig 7 (left) Peter
Stolypin, Prime
Minister 1906-11.

Fig 8 (right)
Gregory
Rasputin.

'Our Friend', as the Tsarina called Rasputin, had peculiar ideas. He was often asked by Nicholas for advice on the appointment of ministers. His method was to 'examine the soul' of a candidate by gazing straight into his eyes. He would then announce whether or not the man possessed the 'Grace of the Lord'. It was possible to improve the quality of one's soul by going on a drinking spree with Rasputin or bribing him beforehand.

The police files were full of reports which revealed the shady side of Rasputin's character. On a November evening, according to one report, Rasputin came home drunk. On hearing that there were two ladies waiting for him he asked, 'Are they pretty? Very pretty? That's good, I need pretty ones.' The Tsarina would believe none of this.

Each morning crowds of people waited to ask for Rasputin's help. Although he readily took money from the rich, he was generous to the poor, and he used his influence to protect the Jews. It was not among the uneducated poor that Rasputin was unpopular; they felt that he was on their side. The nobles hated Rasputin because the Tsar listened to him rather than to them. Able and honest men in the Tsar's service hated Rasputin because he filled the government with his corrupt and often stupid friends who mismanaged the war.

A group of nobles finally planned Rasputin's murder. The night of 30 December 1916 was the chosen time. Rasputin was invited to a downstairs room in the house of Prince Yusupov. Poisoned wine and cakes injected with cyanide of potassium awaited him. Rasputin drank the wine and ate the cakes. Yusupov, his nerves at breaking point, waited for the 'holy man' to collapse. Nothing happened. Hours later Rasputin was feeling lively enough to suggest a trip to a night-club.

23

Yusupov, clutching a revolver behind his back, asked Rasputin to say a prayer: he then shot him in the chest. Rasputin fell and Yusupov's fellow conspirators came rushing in. They left Rasputin for dead, but the Prince was uneasy and returned later to check up. Rasputin rose on all fours and chased him up the stairs, bellowing with rage; another plotter shot Rasputin and he again collapsed. Finally his body was taken by car and thrown in the River Neva. On 1 January when the corpse was recovered by divers there was water in Rasputin's lungs, indicating that he had still been alive when thrown into the river. The Tsar hurried home to comfort his grieving wife but he dared not act against the murderers.

In 1965 Rasputin was still making the headlines. Prince Yusupov and his wife brought a court case against a television producer who had presented a play on the murder. An action-packed film, *Rasputin the Mad Monk,* also appeared at this time.

After Stolypin's death, Nicholas had little luck with his Prime Ministers. During the war, one followed another in a confusing parade, four in two years. The Government made such a mess of organizing Russia for war that people began to think that their mistakes were deliberate. Rumours spread that some ministers were in the pay of Germany.

The transport system almost broke down under the strain of war. Food was short in some areas and there were bread queues in Petrograd. (The capital's name was changed from St. Petersburg at the beginning of the war because this sounded too German.) Many factories were desperately short of raw materials. The cost of living shot up and up until, by the end of 1916, prices were an average of seven times their pre-war level.

During 1916 the Russians again beat the Austrian armies, but they suffered crushing defeats at the hands of the Germans. By January 1917 a million deserters were roaming about in the rear of the Russian army. One general wrote from the front that the troops would welcome a revolution. Nicholas seems to have purposely shut his eyes to the perils which faced him. When Rodzianko, the chairman of the Duma, warned him of the dangers of revolution he remarked, 'Again that fat-bellied Rodzianko has written me a lot of nonsense which I don't even bother to answer.'

In the towns, order was fast breaking down. Early March saw hunger riots in Petrograd: women and factory workers on strike broke into the bakeries. Soldiers of the Petrograd garrison refused to fire on the demonstrators, and some of them shot their own officers instead. Nicholas sent picked troops from the front to re-establish order, but these too became mutinous when they reached the capital. The Tsar's authority had completely collapsed.

Since Russia now had no effective government, the Duma felt that it was their duty to appoint one. This Provisional Government, with Prince Lvov as Prime Minister, first met on 12 March 1917 in the Tauride Palace. The Petrograd Soviet, or council, met in the same building. This soviet was based on the organization set up during the 1905 revolution. It consisted of Social Democrats and Social

Revolutionaries, and was elected mainly by factory workers and soldiers. In effect, Russia now had two new governments. These co-operated to some extent but the Soviet's Order No. 1 told soldiers to obey only those instructions approved by the Soviet.

Nicholas made an attempt to return to the capital, but his train was held up by strikers. Finally, in a railway siding at Pskov, he came face to face with the truth which he had so long avoided. Without the support of the army, the Duma or the people, he was forced to abdicate. At first Nicholas considered naming his son as the new Tsar but his doctor, and the fact that this would have meant separation from the boy, decided him against this. Then he decided on his brother, the Grand Duke Michael; but when Michael heard the news he refused to take the throne unless he was chosen by an elected parliament. For the first time in centuries Russia was without a Tsar.

The almost bloodless March revolution raised hopes that Russia might now be entering a new period of freedom and progress. An American in Petrograd wrote to his wife, 'It has been good to be alive these marvellous days. We can take our hats off to the Russian people; they know how to put great things across.'

Lenin and the November Revolution

Lenin had lived outside Russia since 1907. When the war began in 1914 he realised that it presented great opportunities for the revolutionaries. In his writings he urged the working classes of the warring countries to turn against their own governments; he believed that the war could be transformed into a number of civil wars between the working class and the ruling class in each country. This would have been the beginning of the World Communist Revolution.

When the Russian people had rallied behind the Tsar at the beginning of the war, Lenin had been disappointed. Even in January 1917, when the Russian enthusiasm for war had been destroyed by bloody defeats, Lenin did not realize how close the revolution was. 'We of the older generation may not live to see the decisive battles of this coming revolution', he said.

For some time the German government had been supporting Lenin and other Russian revolutionaries. The Germans had no love for Communism; their aim was to weaken the Russian war effort and if possible to get Russia out of the war. In April 1917 the Germans provided Lenin, his wife and other revolutionaries with a special train to speed them on their journey home. Winston Churchill, no friend of the Bolsheviks, has written, 'They turned upon Russia the most grisly of all weapons. They transported Lenin like a plague bacillus from Switzerland into Russia.'

A great reception had been planned for Lenin when he arrived in Petrograd; a band was playing and a searchlight illuminated the scene. The chairman of the Petrograd Soviet, a Menshevik who supported the Provisional Government, made a speech of welcome. Lenin fidgeted with a bouquet and gazed at the ceiling and at the crowd as if the

Fig 9 Lenin.

speech had nothing to do with him. As soon as it was over Lenin began
to speak himself. He made a bitter attack on the Provisional
Government for continuing the war.

This criticism he later developed in a famous document called the
April Theses, which advocated that the Provisional Government
should be overthrown and its authority given to the workers' councils
which were springing up all over Russia. 'All power to the soviets' was
Lenin's battle cry. The army and the police should be disbanded; land
and industry should belong to the state. Some of Lenin's ideas were not
accepted by many Bolsheviks in the Petrograd Soviet, let alone by the
other members; he was widely regarded as wild and unrealistic. But the
events of the next few months turned the tide in his favour.

The most able member of the Provisional Government was a young lawyer, Alexander Kerensky, who became Prime Minister in July 1917. Now, the Provisional Government was only too aware that it had not been properly elected; its task was to govern Russia until that November, when a general election would take place and Russia's future could be decided by a government elected by the whole of the Russian people. But events did not stand still. Problems arose which would not wait for November.

In many areas the peasants did not wait for Government land reforms, but took the law and the land into their own hands. One old peasant told an official, 'The land's ours now; d'you hear that? If any landlord tries to stop us we'll set fire to the fields.' Peasants' communes in many villages organized the take-over of the land. By July, a thousand large estates had been divided among the peasants.

Workers' councils were also formed in the factories and these made life difficult for the factory owners. The Bolshevik newspaper **Pravda** reported an incident in a wages dispute: 'The behaviour of the owners offended the workers with the result that several members of the management were carried out on stretchers'. There were many strikes, and production declined.

Fig 10 Alexander Kerensky (left), Prime Minister of the Provisional Government in 1917.

The Provisional Government failed to restore discipline in the army; this was their most serious failure. In many units the troops elected soldiers' councils and took orders only from them. They ignored, or at worst murdered, their officers. Peasant soldiers made their way home to claim their share of the noblemen's lands. Despite these difficulties the Provisional Government, nobly but perhaps foolishly, remained in the war at the side of their allies. Kerensky, deciding that a successful offensive would restore the spirit of the Russian army, toured the front, making speeches to the soldiers in a desperate attempt to whip up enthusiasm for a move forward. But when the attack began, some units refused to advance, and the July offensive ended in utter failure. Millions of troops deserted. As Lenin put it, 'The soldiers voted for peace with their feet – they ran away.'

When the news of this defeat reached the capital, violent demonstrations broke out. A huge mob of soldiers and factory workers marched to the Tauride Palace shouting 'Down with the Government, all power to the soviets!' The Bolsheviks were unsure whether the moment for action had arrived, and while they hesitated, the Government was able to restore order. Kerensky now published documents which seemed to prove that Lenin and the Bolsheviks were traitors in the pay of the Germans. A warrant was issued for Lenin's arrest. Disguised as an engine driver, he crossed into Finland on a locomotive's footplate.

At the end of July, Kerensky appointed a Cossack officer, General Kornilov, as commander in chief of the army. Kornilov wanted to abolish soviets in the army and to deal sternly with mutineers. He eventually came to the conclusion that Kerensky was too soft to restore order. Kerensky got wind of Kornilov's plans and dismissed him, but Kornilov refused to resign and ordered soldiers to march on Petrograd. Kerensky prepared to defend the capital, and armed Bolsheviks — the Red Guard — supported him. Railway workers pulled up tracks in order to slow down Kornilov's advance. His own troops lost heart and deserted and Kornilov himself was arrested, although he later escaped.

The Kornilov affair further sapped the public's confidence in the Provisional Government. The Bolsheviks were quick to point out that some members of the government had supported Kornilov's aims. Popular support for the Bolsheviks grew rapidly. The party membership, which numbered 14 000 in February, had risen to 200 000 by October. The Bolsheviks now had a majority in the Petrograd and Moscow Soviets. The Petrograd Soviet set up a Military Revolutionary Committee under Trotsky to plan the overthrow of the government.

By early November 1917 Lenin felt that the time was ripe to seize power. The moment had come for which he had worked for thirty years. 'We must not wait. We may lose everything,' he wrote. Some Bolsheviks were not convinced by Lenin's arguments. They even went so far as to publish their own views, so warning Kerensky of the danger that threatened. The Provisional Government faced the situation with surprising calm, perhaps the calm not of confidence but of tiredness and despair.

Lenin timed the rising for 7 November. Representatives of workers' councils from all over Russia were to meet on 8 November, and though Lenin was by no means sure of their support, he had decided to present them with power whether they wanted it or not.

On the evening of 6 November Lenin, still in disguise, came out of hiding. He joined the meeting of the Military Revolutionary Committee, which was headed by Trotsky and took place in a girls' school where the old signs like 'Ladies Classroom Number 4' were still in position.

By the early hours of 7 November, Trotsky's plans were being put into action. Red Guards and soldiers began to take over the key points in Petrograd and before long railway stations, bridges, power stations and the telephone exchange were in Bolshevik hands.

Kerensky failed to rally soldiers in Petrograd to his side. He borrowed a car belonging to the American Embassy and went in search of loyal troops at the front, but his mission was a failure. Kerensky escaped from Russia and eventually went to the U.S.A., where he lived until his death in 1970.

At the time of the rising, members of the Provisional Government were holding a meeting at the Winter Palace. This huge building, covering several hectares, was guarded by a few hundred officer-cadets and a 'Women's Death Battalion', so called because its members had sworn to fight to the death against the Germans. In the evening the Bolsheviks began to attack the palace but it was not badly damaged. However, they managed to work their way into the building, and early on 8 November they arrested the Provisional Government. Now factory worker K. P. Ivanov felt safe to take off his wig and appear again as Lenin.

During the rising there was little violence. Shops and cinemas stayed open; most people went to work as usual, and not many realized what was happening. The whole operation went off quickly and smoothly. As a French observer put it, the Provisional Government was overthrown before it could say 'Ouch!'

Yet Lenin's position was still very shaky. Petrograd was only the capital of a vast country, and both inside and outside Russia anti-Bolsheviks prepared to do battle.

SUMMARY – Chapter 2

KARL MARX AND COMMUNISM
Marx's Communist Manifesto of 1848 urged the workers of the world to
overthrow their rulers and run their governments themselves. They
would then work for the common good and receive what they needed
without payment.

LENIN'S EARLY LIFE
Lenin (Vladimir Ulyanov) was born in 1870, the son of an education
officer. His brother was executed for attempting to assassinate the
Tsar. Lenin became a Communist, was arrested and exiled to Siberia.
He later lived in western Europe, where he met Trotsky and wrote for
the revolutionary paper *Iskra*. Lenin helped to form the Social
Democratic Party, which aimed to overthrow the Tsar. When the Party
split he became the leader of the Bolshevik group.

WAR BETWEEN RUSSIA AND JAPAN (1904-1905)
Russia and Japan both wanted Manchuria, which belonged to the weak
Chinese empire. In 1904 the Japanese attacked the Russian base of Port
Arthur and the next year defeated a Russian army at Mukden. The
Russian fleet was sunk at Tsushima. The Japanese gained land with
the peace treaty of 1905. The Tsar lost the confidence of the Russian
people.

THE 1905 REVOLUTION
The workers of St. Petersburg, led by Father Gapon, petitioned the
Tsar for better conditions and for an end to the war. Soldiers opened
fire, killing 600 of them. Risings then occurred all over Russia. There
were mutinies in the armed forces. The Social Democrats were slow to
act but set up a workers' council (soviet) in St. Petersburg. The
revolution ended in December after Nicholas had promised to set up a
Parliament (Duma), but the new voting system favoured the rich and
real power still remained in the Tsar's hande.

STOLYPIN AND THE DUMA
The first two Dumas were hostile to the Tsar and were dismissed. A
third Duma, elected after the workers had been deprived of their votes,

lasted five years. Stolypin, made Prime Minister in 1906, tried to gain the support of the peasants. He ended land payments and permitted peasants to build up individual farms. New lands were farmed in Siberia. The good effect of these reforms was lessened by the growth of population. Stolypin also encouraged industry and education. He was assassinated in 1911.

THE FIRST WORLD WAR AND THE MARCH REVOLUTION
Serbia, whose people were Slavs, like the Russians, was invaded by Austria. Russia, supported by France and Britain, declared war on Austria and Germany. In 1914 the Russians defeated the Austrians but were beaten by the Germans at Tannenberg. After further defeats, Tsar Nicholas went to the front to command the army and the Tsarina, advised by the monk Rasputin, ruled Russia. Rasputin used his influence to promote his friends in the Government. He was murdered by a group of nobles in 1916. The Government organized the war badly. There were shortages of food and weapons. Further defeats occurred. There were strikes and soldiers became disloyal. In March 1917 the Tsar was forced to abdicate and the Duma set up a Provisional Government. Socialists set up a rival organization, the Petrograd Soviet.

LENIN AND THE NOVEMBER REVOLUTION
Lenin was still living abroad when the war began. In April 1917, the Germans sent him home in a special train. He criticized the Provisional Government for continuing the war and demanded that power be transferred to workers' councils. In many areas peasants' communes took over the land and workers' councils were formed in factories. Soldiers' councils undermined the authority of the Provisional Government, which was headed by Kerensky. With the failure of the July offensive and the mutiny of General Kornilov, the position of the Kerensky government became desperate. The Bolsheviks grew rapidly in strength and took control of the Petrograd Soviet, which set up the Military Revolutionary Committee under Trotsky. On 7 November 1917 Trotsky's plans were carried out and the Provisional Government was easily overthrown.

Lenin: Civil War and Reconstruction

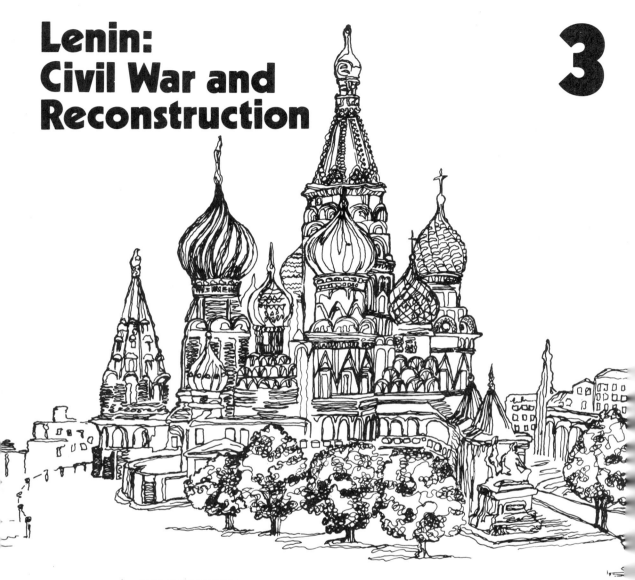

FIRST MOVES

While the defenders of the Winter Palace were still exchanging shots with the Bolsheviks, Lenin rose to address the Congress of Soviets meeting in the Smolny Girls' School. He was received with roars of applause. John Reed, an American journalist and a friend of Lenin, was there and described him: ' . . . a short stocky figure with a big head set down in his shoulders, bald and bulging. Little eyes, a snubbish nose, wide generous mouth and heavy chin . . . in shabby clothes, his trousers much too long for him. Unimpressive to be the idol of a mob.' It was not Lenin's appearance but his skill as a speaker which captured the crowd.

In his speech to the Congress, Lenin introduced two important measures, the Decrees on Peace and Land. The Peace Decree called on all countries at war to stop fighting and to negotiate a just peace without conquests. The Land Decree stated that all land, including that owned by the Church, now belonged to the State. It should be taken over by the village soviets and shared among the peasants, and this in fact had already been done in many areas. There were other sweeping changes: committees of workers were set up to supervise factories; banks came under Government ownership; the old system of law courts was abolished and justice was administered by groups of workers. Some newspapers were closed down and others were censored.

Lenin used the Bolshevik majority in the Congress of Soviets to keep Mensheviks and Social Revolutionaries out of the new government. The Council of People's Commissars, a sort of Cabinet of ministers chosen by the Congress, were all Bolsheviks. Lenin became President and Trotsky Foreign Minister.

Not all London newspapers gave the Bolshevik Revolution the main headline. Few foreigners expected the new government to last long. In Petrograd itself, bank workers refused to take the Communists' orders and went on strike. Neither telephone girls nor railwaymen accepted Lenin's government. On 11 November, officer cadets seized the telephone exchange and were driven out only after bitter fighting. Despite these setbacks, the Bolsheviks strengthened their grip on the capital, and eventually the workers on strike ran out of money and drifted back to work.

Moscow fell to Bolshevik troops after a week of fierce fighting. All over Russia, Bolsheviks in the villages, towns and army camps worked to build up support for the new government, trying to form Bolshevik majorities in the local soviets. Sometimes they were successful; often they were not.

The Constituent Assembly, January 1918

Meanwhile arrangements went ahead for the election on 25 November of the first Parliament to be chosen by the ordinary Russian people — the Consituent Assembly. Despite all their efforts, the Bolsheviks polled only about 25 per cent of the votes. The Social Revolutionaries kept their support among the peasants and gained over half the votes; they were by far the largest party.

Lenin delayed the opening of the Constituent Assembly until 18 January. When that long-awaited day dawned, his plans were carefully laid. On arriving at the hall in the Tauride Palace, the representatives found a hostile audience of armed Bolshevik guards. Lenin made sure that the proceedings were more like a pantomime than a Parliament. A Social Revolutionary was chosen as President, but his opening speech was interrupted by boos and cat-calls. Only the Bolshevik speakers were listened to in silence. When the President referred to the people's wishes, a soldier pointed a rifle at him and yelled, 'A bullet through his head, that's what they want!'' Pictures were wrenched from the walls, chairs and tables were overturned. 'Stop the session! We've had enough!' roared the soldiers. A sailor climbed on to the platform and said that he had been ordered to clear the hall: the guards were tired and they were going to cut off the electricity. Finally, at two o'clock in the morning, the meeting broke up in confusion.

The Constituent Assembly was not opposed to most of the Bolsheviks' plans — they had approved an armistice with Germany and a land policy similar to Lenin's — but they would not agree to a government controlled by the Bolsheviks. The next day soldiers prevented the Assembly's members from entering the Tauride Palace. Lenin believed that it was the Communist party's destiny to build a new Russia from the confusion of military defeat and economic chaos which paralysed the country. No opposition, not even that of the freely elected representatives of the Russian people, was allowed to stand in his way.

On 20 December the Bolsheviks set up a secret police, the **Cheka.** This organization was a descendant of the Tsarist secret police, whose files it used. Some members of the Cheka were recruited from criminals released at the time of the revolution. They took part in the looting and murders which were then frequent in Petrograd; the Cheka removed many of the Bolsheviks enemies. Its violent methods were strongly criticized both in Russia and abroad, but Lenin believed the Cheka was essential to keep the Communists in power.

The Treaty of Brest — Litovsk, March 1918

On 21 November Lenin sent orders to General Dukhonin, the Russian Commander-in-Chief, to arrange a ceasefire with the Germans. When the General, who had been appointed by Kerensky, refused he was replaced by a Bolshevik, and later was murdered by his own troops. Russia's allies, Britain, France and the U.S.A., were furious with the Bolsheviks for seeking a separate peace.

Trotsky led the Russian representatives in the peace negotiations at Brest-Litovsk in Poland. The delegation included a soldier, a sailor, a worker and a moujik. The peasant, a passer-by picked up at the last moment, puzzled the German officials. He drank vast quantities of alcohol at receptions but added nothing to the peace discussions. Trotsky dragged out the talks as long as possible, hoping that Communist revolutions in Europe would be sparked off by the one in Russia. Bolshevik agents were particularly active in Germany trying to persuade the workers to overthrow their government. Trotsky's plans failed. The Germans became impatient with Russian delaying tactics and insisted on a reply to their very demanding peace terms. Trotsky advocated the policy of Neither Peace nor War, by which he meant that the Russians refused the German demands, but the Red Army would not fight. The Germans' patience snapped and they resumed their advance. The Russians moved the capital from Petrograd to Moscow as a prelude to continuing the war.

The Bolshevik leaders were divided over the German peace terms. Lenin insisted that Russia needed peace whatever the cost. He threatened to resign and in the end his view just prevailed. On 3 March 1918, the German and Russian delegations signed the Treaty of Brest-Litovsk. Russia's losses were enormous — she gave up a quarter of her land, a third of her population and half her industry — but the Bolsheviks hoped that Communists might yet take over in Germany and restore Russia's lost lands.

Some Russians regarded the peace as a betrayal and turned to violence. On 6 July the German Ambassador was murdered. On 30 August, as Lenin was leaving a meeting, a young Social Revolutionary, Dora Kaplan, stepped forward. She fired two bullets into Lenin at close range and he collapsed. One shot broke his left shoulder, the other penetrated his neck from left to right and damaged a lung. Doctors reported, 'If the bullet had deviated one millimetre in either direction, Vladimir Ilyich would of course already be dead.' Lenin took the incident very calmly, and after a month's convalescence he was ready for work again, the bullets still lodged in his body. Dora Kaplan was executed.

CIVIL WAR

Meanwhile, the Bolsheviks were struggling to extend their power over all Russia. In the chaos created by war and the collapse of Tsarist rule, independent governments had sprung up in many parts of the country. Although these were known collectively as 'Whites' to distinguish them from the Bolshevik 'Reds', these governments usually acted independently of each other. The Whites represented a wide range of political beliefs; some wished to restore the rights of property owners but others were Socialists. All Whites were anti-Bolshevik but very few wanted the Tsar back in power. **White Armies** were supported by the Allies — Britain, France, U.S.A. and Japan — who hoped to use the Whites to keep the war going against Germany in the east.

The **Red Army,** led by Trotsky, at first consisted of volunteers who elected their own officers, but this system failed because of a shortage of recruits and poor discipline. Young men were then conscripted into the Red Army and thousands of officers from the old Tsarist army were employed. Most of these officers were far from being keen Communists and to ensure their loyalty they were constantly accompanied by Bolsheviks armed with pistols.

The first challenge to the Bolsheviks came from the Don Province in South Russia. There the Cossacks had set up an independent state and recruited an army led by General Kornilov. In December 1917 fighting broke out in the area. The Red Army was victorious and Kornilov died in the struggle. But the Cossack army re-formed under General Denikin and launched a vigorous attack in the spring of 1919. The British, who had their eyes on the oil wells of South Russia and had established bases on the Black Sea, now sent military supplies to the White army. Denkin's army rolled northwards and by October was three hundred kilometres from Moscow. Yet this advance was badly organized, even chaotic. Officers grew rich by selling military stores; soldiers gave up fighting and went home when they had collected enough booty. Most serious of all, Denikin's army roused the hatred of the peasants by robbery, brutality, and threatening to restore the former landowners. Some of the peasants formed into guerilla bands and attacked Denikin's supply columns. The further Denikin's army advanced the weaker it became, and finally it crumbled away under the pressure of counter-attacks by the Red Army. The remnants of the force were eventually evacuated from the Crimea by British ships.

In Siberia another danger threatened the Bolsheviks. During the war many Czecho-Slovak soldiers who had been forced to serve in the Austrian army were taken prisoner by the Russians, and these Czechs proved willing to take up arms against their former rulers. They were formed into the Czech Legion, which by 1918 was about 40,000 strong. Before making peace with Germany, the Russians had agreed to send the Czechs for service in France. This meant a long train journey to Vladivostock before embarking on ship. Disputes occurred between the Bolsheviks and the Czechs over the supply of rolling stock and other matters. When the Russians tried to disarm the Czechs in March 1918 fighting broke out, and in a few weeks a line of towns on the Trans-Siberian Railway stretching from the Volga to the Pacific coast was in Czech hands. Allied troops, mainly American and Japanese, landed at Vladivostock to help the Czechs. They also gave their support to Admiral Kolchak, who had set up a White government in Siberia and hopefully assumed the title 'Supreme Ruler of All Russia'.

These events decided the fate of Nicholas II and his family, who were being held under close guard by the Bolsheviks at Ekaterinburg (now Sverdlovsk) in Western Siberia. On 16 July 1918 a Czech force was advancing on the town. In the late evening the Tsar, with his sick son in his arms, the Tsarina and her four daughters were ordered down into the cellar of the house. An execution order was read to them and they fell under a volley of rifle shots. With them died their family doctor, three personal servants and even their spaniel, 'Jimmy'. The bodies were cut up, soaked in acid, burned and thrown down a disused iron mine.

Kolchak prepared a great offensive to the west backed by the supplies that the Allies were pouring into Vladivostock. The story of this campaign is in many ways similar to Denikin's in South Russia. There was the same brutality towards the peasants, the same corruption and selfishness among the officers. A British soldier wrote: 'I think most of us were secretly in sympathy with the Bolsheviks after our experience with the corruption and cowardice of the other side. It was revolting to see wounded men dragging their way from station to hospital over dirty streets for perhaps a mile or two while officers rode scornfully by in *droshkies,* or motor cars.'

Kolchak's advance, which began in January 1919, had burnt itself out by late April when he had reached Samara. A Red Army counter-attack sent his forces reeling back to his capital of Omsk. The Bolsheviks captured so much British equipment in the town that they sent a telegram of thanks to the British general. Kolchak fell into the hands of the Red Army and was executed.

Only the two most important areas contested in the Civil War have been described. The Red Army fought many other campaigns and by

1922 the last of the White armies had been defeated and the last foreign troops had left Russian soil. The Allies had less interest in supporting the Whites after the defeat of Germany in November 1918 and their people were sick of war. In fact the Allied intervention had the effect of encouraging the White armies to over-extend themselves and in the long run probably did them more harm than good.

The Red Army's successes in the Civil War owed much to Trotsky's dynamic leadership. He toured the front in a special train organizing and encouraging the troops, and used ruthless measures to transform what he once called a 'flabby mass' into an efficient fighting force. On one occasion when a whole regiment deserted and seized a Volga river boat to escape, one man in ten was shot dead as a punishment.

WAR COMMUNISM (1918-1921)

In November 1917 the Bolsheviks took over a country whose industries were collapsing under the strain of war. Agricultural production was declining and the breakdown of the railways made it difficult to distribute food. The cost of living was five times higher than it had been a year earlier.

Lenin was given no breathing space before the Civil War flung the economy into further chaos. In 1918 the Communists endeavoured to maintain supplies for the Red Army by a policy of close Government control of industry and agriculture. This policy became known as 'War Communism'.

The system of workers' supervision of factories had not been a success. The workers had proved more interested in settling old scores with the management and in improving their own conditions than in increasing production. All factories now came under direct Government control. The Government sent workers to where they were needed. Strikers were punished as enemy agents.

Since money was worthless, workers were paid in goods and services. Food was rationed and manual workers received most, a group called 'non-working citizens', which included all those of doubtful loyalty, receiving least of all. The latter could exist only by selling personal possessions to buy food on the 'black market'.

Despite all the Bolsheviks could do, millions of factory workers joined relations in the countryside, where there was more food; half the workers left the towns between 1917 and 1920. Production slumped disastrously to only about one seventh of pre-war levels. To make matters worse Russia was blockaded by the Allies until 1920, so goods could not be brought in from outside.

Peasants were ordered to sell all their surplus grain to the state to feed the townsfolk. But as the towns were producing nothing for them to buy, the peasants grew only enough for themselves, reducing the area of land under crops by half. The Bolsheviks were now forced into desperate measures to combat the food shortage. Raiding parties were sent out from the towns to seize stores of food hidden in the villages. In some areas, as part of a long-term plan, peasants were encouraged or compelled to combine their plots to form large farms. It was not Communist policy to leave some twenty million peasants happily but inefficiently tending their own small farms.

The strict measures of War Communism made the Bolsheviks unpopular with many workers. Throughout 1920 there were peasant uprisings in which newly disbanded soldiers often took part, and early in 1921 there was a wave of strikes in Petrograd. These sparked off a mutiny in the naval base on the nearby island of Kronstadt. Among the rebels' demands were 'freedom of speech and press for all workers . . . the abolition of the specially privileged position of the Communist Party . . . full rights for the peasants to do what they like with their land.' For three weeks the mutineers held out before Kronstadt was captured by Red Army men advancing through blinding snow over the thick ice. Hundreds of the rebels were shot, but Lenin knew that this was not enough. He spoke of the Kronstadt revolt as 'the flash which lit up reality.' Although the Government had the loyal support of thousands of Communist Party members they had, in Lenin's words, 'failed to convince the broad masses.'

Faced with the hostility of the workers and the collapse of industry, Lenin decided on a 'New Economic Policy'. This is described later.

Famine, 1920-1923

Russia's food shortage was aggravated by widespread drought in 1920 and 1921. The harvest failed completely in south-east Russia and about 50 million people faced starvation. The Russian Government sent what help it could to the stricken area. Foreign organizations, in particular the American Relief Administration, fed millions of Russians. But all this was not enough to prevent the death of five million people.

An American relief worker described his experiences: he told of 'waiting children who fought with dogs for crusts of bread'; he had 'seen men arrested for cannibalism; they had killed and eaten a young boy.' An old peasant showed an American traveller his bread: ' . . . a greenish-purply mess. Traces of flour embedded in patches of clay and held together by fibres of grass and weeds. I tried to eat a little but I could not swallow it.' Others ate dirt and bark. When their energy failed they flopped down and waited quietly for death.

The new economic policy

Lenin had the strength of character to face facts, however unpleasant they were. In March 1921 he said, 'We are in a condition of such poverty, ruin and exhaustion . . . that everything must be set aside to increase production.' The aim of the New Economic Policy was to give Russia a breathing space in which she could restore prosperity.

In the countryside the persecution of rich peasants stopped. The confiscation of grain was ended and replaced by a grain tax of about 10 per cent of total production. The peasants were allowed to sell on the

Fig 11 Starving children at Samara during the famine of 1922.

open market whatever produce they had to spare. Once the drought was over food production rose; the harvest of 1923 was a good one.

The Government also relaxed control over industry. Small factories and shops could be set up under private ownership. The State kept what Lenin called the 'commanding heights' of the economy: large factories, mines, transport, banks and foreign trade. In fact, seven-eighths of industrial workers were still employed by the Government. Forced labour was ended and people were paid in money instead of goods. Foreign countries were encouraged to trade with Russia.

A visitor reported what a difference the N.E.P. made to life in Moscow: 'Shops and restaurants are being re-opened . . . traffic has increased tenfold. The city is full of peasants selling fruit, vegetables.' Shady clubs which offered gambling, girls and drugs were allowed to flourish, provided that they paid a tax to the Government on their profits.

Not surprisingly, the New Economic Policy was bitterly resented by some Communists, who saw lulaks and merchants becoming rich while many workers were poor or unemployed. The joke went round that N.E.P. stood for 'New Exploitation of the People'. Lenin patiently rejected this criticism. He had not abandoned Communism, he had delayed it for the sake of national survival. Lenin said in his last public speech in Novemver 1922, 'We are now retreating . . . in order to get a better run for our longer leap forward.'

Social changes in the 1920s

Lenin's government made sweeping social changes. More hospitals were built and medical care was free. Marriage laws were relaxed and divorce could be had for the asking. Women were given the same opportunities as men in education and careers. Even before the Revolution, Russia had led the world in providing university education for women, and now the expansion of education was helped by the large number of well-qualified women available.

Despite economic difficulties, more schools were built. The strict classroom discipline of Tsarist days was abandoned. In order to arouse the pupils' interest and sense of responsibility, they were often allowed to organize the school routine themselves. At the worst, this led to teachers struggling for survival among unruly pupils; but at the best it brought a spirit of friendliness and co-operation into the classroom. Universities were opened to the intelligent child from a working-class family but closed to the child of a former factory manager or landowner.

Religion was permitted, but strongly discouraged, by the Communists. Many churches were turned into schools or warehouses and priests were placed in the lowest group of non-working citizens.

Foreign Affairs, 1918-1923

After Germany's surrender to the Allies in November 1918, the Treaty of Brest-Litovsk became only a worthless sheet of paper. Nevertheless the Allies, who were supporting the Whites in the Civil War, did not permit Russia to re-occupy all her lost territories. To prevent the spread of Communism, they supported the setting up of independent states on Russia's western borders. These included Finland, Poland and the small Baltic states of Estonia, Latvia and Lithuania (see the map above).

In order to bring about world-wide Communism as soon as possible the Russians set up the **Communist International (Comintern)** in 1919. Its task was to spread Communist ideas among the working classes abroad and to plan for the overthrow of the governments of Capitalist countries. The Comintern was useful in bringing foreign Communists under Russian control; Comintern agents were at first very active in Germany. However, it failed to bring about successful Communist revolutions, and made foreign governments deeply distrustful of Russia.

A dispute arose over the Polish frontier with Russia. In April 1920, encouraged by France, the Polish army advanced deep into the

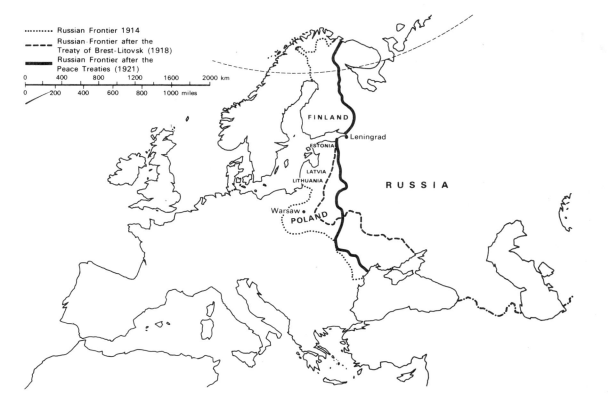

FINLAND

Leningrad

ESTONIA

LATVIA

LITHUANIA

RUSSIA

Warsaw

POLAND

Map 4 Russia in 1921

Ukraine. This triumph was short-lived and before long cavalry of the Red Army were in the outskirts of Warsaw. For a time Lenin saw dazzling prospects unfolding. The advance might be continued into Germany, where Communists were rapidly gaining influence in the confusion and despair which followed defeat. But the Red Army had over-extended itself and was pushed back by the Poles. The Treaty of Riga of March 1921 gave large border areas to Poland.

Despite the efforts of the Comintern, Russia was still the only country with a Communist government in 1922. Russia felt she was surrounded by enemies and needed a friend in a hostile world. Germany too wanted a foreign alliance to strengthen her weak position after the war. The two outcasts of Europe, Germany and Russia, after talks at Rapallo in Italy, made an agreement in April 1922. They agreed to cancel all debts and to co-operate to build up the industries of both countries. One section of the treaty was kept secret: this permitted Germany to set up in Russia factories to produce poison gas, aircraft and tanks as well as military training schools.

In 1923 the Russians found another ally, this time in the east; Dr Sun Yat-sen, the Chinese leader, asked for Russian help to strengthen his position in the country. The Chinese emperor had been overthrown by a revolution led by Sun Yat-sen's Nationalist Party in 1911. However, large areas of China were still held by local war-lords who would not

41

accept Sun Yat-sen's government. A team of experts, led by Michael Borodin, went to China. Borodin soon gained great influence in both military and economic affairs, and for a while it seemed that his efforts might lead to China becoming a Communist state.

Lenin's illness and death

On 26 March 1922 Lenin suffered a stroke. A German specialist who examined him had little doubt of the cause; Lenin had been working sixteen hours a day for thirty years. After a period of convalescence, Lenin again took up his duties as Prime Minister. A second stroke in December paralysed an arm and a leg. From his sick-bed he continued to take part in Russia's government but his influence grew less.

A third stroke on 9 March 1923 ended Lenin's political career. The great leader whose words had changed history lost the power of speech. 'Vot!' ('That's it!') was all he could say clearly. In the summer Lenin's condition improved; he was fitted with special shoes and learned to walk with the aid of a stick. On one occasion he summoned up the energy to visit for the last time his office in the Kremlin.

Lenin died after a final stroke on 21 January 1924. Despite the bitterly cold weather, hundreds of thousands came to file past his coffin in the Hall of Columns in Moscow. Petrograd was renamed Leningrad in his honour and Lenin's body was embalmed and placed under a glass case in a mausoleum in Moscow's Red Square. Every day a constant stream of visitors passes in front of the architect of modern Russia. Lenin would have disapproved of the mausoleum and all the hero-worship. He was not a vain man.

Russian Communists regard Lenin's writings as the inspired and lasting truth, in much the same way as Christians regard the Bible. A recent Russian poster bore the inscription, 'Lenin Lived, Lenin Lives, Lenin Shall Always Live.'

The life of Lenin

(Vladimir Ilyich Ulyanov) *A SUMMARY*

1870	Born in south Russia son of a school inspector.
1887	Became a Communist revolutionary after his brother's execution.
1887	Expelled from university for revolutionary views.
1896	Imprisoned and exiled to Siberia, where he married in 1898.
1900	Went to live abroad where he published the newspaper *Iskra* and planned for revolution.
1903	Became the leader of the Bolshevik group of the Social Democratic Party.
1905	Temporary return to Russia to join in the Revolution.
1917	Returned to Russia after the Tsar's abdication and led the Bolshevik overthrow of the Provisional Government.
1917–18	Took land and factories from their owners and gave them to the peasants and workers.
1918	Treaty of Brest-Litovsk with Germany.
1918	Survived attempt at assassination.
1918–21	Civil war with the Whites and foreign armies. Strict control of agriculture and industry under War Communism.
1919	Formed the Comintern to spread Communism abroad.
1921	Introduced the New Economic Policy to revive Russia's economy.

SUMMARY – Chapter 3

FIRST MOVES
The Bolsheviks formed the new government. Lenin became President and Trotsky Foreign Minister. They made sweeping changes. The Peace Decree called for an end to the war. The Land Decree stated that all land belonged to the State but should be shared among peasants. Factories came under workers' control. The Bolshevik troops captured Moscow but most of Russia was outside their control.

THE CONSTITUENT ASSEMBLY, JANUARY 1918
The Bolsheviks polled only 25 per cent of the votes for Russia's first freely elected Parliament. The Social Revolutionaries, the party of the peasants, had over 50 per cent but the Bolsheviks broke up the Assembly's meeting. The Cheka (secret police) was set up to deal with anti-Bolsheviks.

THE TREATY OF BREST-LITOVSK, MARCH 1918
Despite the anger of Russia's allies, the Bolsheviks made peace with Germany. Russia lost a quarter of her land and half her industries. This caused widespread dismay and an attempt was made to assassinate Lenin.

CIVIL WAR (1917-1922)
The Bolshevik Red Army had to oppose several White Armies. These were independent of each other and represented widely differing political views. The Whites were supported by Britain, France, U.S.A. and Japan. A Cossack army in the south led by Kornilov and Denikin, the Czech Legion and Kolchak's army in Siberia were all defeated by the Red Army under Trotsky's vigorous leadership. There was brutality by Reds and Whites and much corruption among the White armies. Bolsheviks executed the Tsar and his family during the fighting.

WAR COMMUNISM (1918-1921)
Industry and agriculture were breaking down under the stress of war. To ensure supplies for the Red Army, food was rationed and a strict government control over factories and farms was begun. This was called War Communism. Because of the food shortage, half of the

factory workers left the towns and production slumped. The Government forced peasants to hand over food for the towns. The policy of War Communism provoked strikes among town workers and peasants and a naval mutiny at Kronstadt.

FAMINE 1920-1923
Drought brought famine to south-east Russia. Despite foreign help five million people died.

THE NEW ECONOMIC POLICY
Lenin realized War Communism had failed and launched the N.E.P. as a temporary measure to restore Russia's economy. He relaxed control over agriculture and industry permitting private ownership of small factories and shops. All large enterprises remained in Government hands. Some Communists were critical of the N.E.P., but when it ended in 1928 Russia was producing more than she had in pre-war years.

SOCIAL CHANGES IN THE 1920s
Divorce was made easy. Many schools were built and the strict class discipline of Tsarist times was abandoned. University education was extended. Hospitals were built and medical care was free. Religion was discouraged and many churches closed.

FOREIGN AFFAIRS 1918-1923
After Germany's defeat the Allies gave Russia back some of her lost lands, setting up independent Baltic States to seal off Russia, and Communism from the West. A war with Poland (1920-21) resulted in Russia losing more land. The Bolsheviks set up the Communist International (Comintern) in 1919 to spread Communism throughout the world. Its main achievement was to bring foreign Communists under Russian control. In 1922 Germany and Russia made an agreement at Rapallo to co-operate in trade and military matters. Borodin was sent to help the leader Sun Yat-sen strengthen his position in China.

LENIN'S ILLNESS AND DEATH
Lenin suffered a stroke in 1922 and after a period of failing health died in January 1924. His body was placed in a mausoleum in Moscow's Red Square.

Stalin: Economic Revolution

YOUTH AND EARLY CAREER

Joseph Djugashvili, later known as Stalin, was born on 21 December 1879 in a two-roomed hut. His father was a cobbler; his mother had to work as a washer-woman to make up the family income. They lived in the village of Gori in Georgia, South Russia. Joseph was their fourth child but the first to survive infancy, though when he was six he did have a severe attack of smallpox which left his face pock-marked for the rest of his life.

When Joseph was eleven his father died. Mrs. Djugashvili, poor and illiterate herself, had great ambitions for her only son. Somehow she saved the money to send him to the village school. The lessons there were in Russian, a language foreign to young Joseph. Georgia had been

Fig 12 Joseph
Djugashvili
(Stalin) as a
revolutionary
leader in 1912.

an independent kingdom and Georgian children hated having to use
Russian, the official language of the Tsar's empire. They sometimes
showed their feelings by attacking teachers and burning down schools.
Joseph, however, was a quiet and hardworking pupil. On leaving Gori
school, he was given a scholarship to attend a training college for
priests in Tiflis, the capital of Georgia.

The college was run by monks and discipline was strict. A student
wrote, 'Locked in day and night within barrack walls, we felt like
prisoners who must spend years there without being guilty of anything'.
The relationship between monks and students was usually most

47

unfriendly. One boy who was expelled came back and murdered the Principal, and a student strike just before Joseph's arrival had led to eighty-seven expulsions. Stalin later said that it was the oppressive atmosphere of the college, together with his own background of poverty that had made him a Communist. Despite all the college's efforts, or more likely because of them, the pupils were full of revolutionary ideas. Joseph joined a Communist group in the town and spread Marx's ideas among workmen in the slums. A college report on his behaviour said, 'Djugashvili is generally disrespectful and rude towards persons in authority.' In 1899 he was expelled.

Joseph became a disciple of Lenin after reading his newspaper *Iskra* which was smuggled into Georgia. During the next few years he often changed his name to confuse the police. He called himself Koba, Vassil, Nanovich, Cato and Stalin ('Man of Steel'). In 1901 he was staying with an old Moslem and producing a revolutionary newspaper on printing presses hidden in the house. Stalin's comrades came disguised as Moslem women and concealed the papers beneath their long robes and veils. In April 1902 the police caught up with him and after a period in jail he was sent to Siberia. He escaped and returned to Tiflis. Stalin married in 1904 but his wife died a year later of tuberculosis, and he did not remarry until 1919.

Stalin became increasingly important among revolutionary groups in south Russia. He sided with Lenin when the Social Democratic Party split into Bolshevik and Menshevik factions. Just before the Revolution of 1905 he wrote 'The time has come to destroy the Tsarist government and destroy it we shall!' During the same year he met Lenin for the first time at a conference in Finland. After organizing strikes in the oil-town of Baku, Stalin again fell into the hands of the police. A fellow prisoner spoke of Stalin's strong nerves, which were to sustain him throughout a troubled life; he would read a text book or settle down for a peaceful sleep while other prisoners were being hanged in the yard outside. In 1907 Stalin planned a daring raid on a carriage belonging to the State Bank in Tiflis and the money went into Bolshevik Party funds. Between 1902 and 1913 he was imprisoned and exiled six times. Five times he escaped.

At the time of the revolution in March 1917 Stalin was in exile, but after being freed he went to Petrograd, where he became Editor of the Communist newspaper *Pravda*. After Lenin's return in April he worked with him.

Stalin was not one of the main architects of the November revolution but afterwards he was made Commissar of Nationalities. His job was a very difficult one: to persuade the **minority races** of Russia, such as the Georgians and the Ukranians that Bolshevik rule would be in their interest. These races had been oppressed under the Tsar, and the Bolsheviks now declared that all races would be able to choose whether to stay in Russia or to form independent countries. One of Stalin's first tasks was to arrange the independence of Finland. But this policy was abandoned when it seemed likely to lead to the break-up of the old Russian empire. Stalin himself ordered the Red Army to march into his native Georgia to overthrow the Menshevik government there.

Although forced to remain under Communist control, the minority races were allowed to use their own languages and to follow their own customs; at this time they fared better than under the Tsar.

During the Civil War Stalin went to Tsaritsyn on the Volga to organize the transport of food to starving Moscow; this he managed to do despite the activities of a White army in the area. A few years later Tsaritsyn was renamed Stalingrad in his honour. Stalin became involved in a dispute over military operations at Tsaritsyn with Trotsky, the Commander-in-Chief of the Red Army. Behind the quarrel lay personal jealousy. Both Stalin and Trotsky were brilliant organisers; but Trotsky became popular as a stirring speaker, while Stalin's speeches were long-winded and boring. Stalin resented being overshadowed by a man who had not joined the Bolshevik Party until 1917. As the war went on, Stalin was sent from one trouble spot to another to organize the Bolshevik forces. In 1919 he achieved an outstanding success in holding Petrograd against a White Army.

Stalin takes over

Stalin's ability and energy and his willingness to undertake tedious work brought him new appointments. In 1919 he became Commissar of the Workers' and Peasants' Inspectorate, which checked the efficiency and honesty of the Government Departments, and in 1922 he was made General Secretary of the Communist Party, an event which did not seem very important at the time.

Stalin used these posts to build up his power. The process was very gradual and hardly anyone was aware of it at first, although the dying Lenin realized the danger. He wrote in a letter: 'Having become General Secretary, Comrade Stalin has concentrated boundless power in his hands, and I am not certain that he can always use the power with sufficient caution . . . I propose to the comrades to consider a means of removing Stalin from that post and appoint another person . . . more patient, more loyal, more polite.' This letter was read to the Central Committee of the Communist Party after Lenin's death. Stalin boldly offered to resign, but his friends managed to persuade the others that Lenin's mind had been clouded by illness. The letter was kept secret until after Stalin's death.

Trotsky was Stalin's chief rival for the leadership of the Communist Party when Lenin died. Behind their personal conflict lay disagreement over the future course of Russia's development. Trotsky stressed the need to organize Communist revolutions abroad. Stalin pushed this issue into the background; he wanted to concentrate on building Communism in Russia first of all. Stalin called this policy 'Socialism in one country'. He realized that after the misery of the war against Germany and the Civil War the Russian people wanted peace. Among Lenin's speeches, Stalin found a quotation to back up his new policy: 'We have sufficient territory and sufficient natural wealth to provide everybody . . . with adequate means of existence.'

Stalin used his key position of General Secretary of the Communist Party to promote his own supporters. Trotsky was gradually squeezed out. In 1925 he was forced to give up his post as Minister of War; two years later he was expelled from the Communist Party together with eighty followers; and in 1929 Trotsky was deported from Russia.

DEVELOPMENT OF INDUSTRY

In order to put into practice Stalin's policy of 'Socialism in one country', it was necessary to develop Russia's industries and bring them all under state ownership. As Stalin put the situation: 'We are fifty or a hundred years behind the advanced countries. We must make up this leeway in ten years. Either we do it or they crush us.' Heavy industry which provided the basis for military strength was to be given priority over the production of consumer goods.

After two years of study, the Government Planning Organization produced a detailed scheme for the development of industry and agriculture over the next five years. This plan was very ambitious: for example, the production of coal, oil, iron and steel were to be trebled. The first Five Year Plan ran from 1928 to 1932 and was followed by a second one ending in 1937.

Development of Soviet Industry 1928-1940

	1928	1940
Coal	35 500 000 tonnes	165 900 000 tonnes
Crude steel	4 300 000 tonnes	18 300 000 tonnes
Crude oil	11 600 000 tonnes	31 100 000 tonnes
Cement	1 800 000 tonnes	5 700 000 tonnes
Electricity	5 000 000 000 KW hours	48 000 000 000 KW hours
Cotton fabrics	2 678 000 000 metres	3 954 000 000 metres
Clocks and watches	900 000	2 800 000
Tins or bottles of goods	125 000 000	1 113 000 000
Motor vehicles	700	145 400
All industry (production in 1913 = 100)	132	852

Development of Soviet Agriculture 1928-1940

	1928	1940
Grain	92 200 000 hectares	110 500 000 hectares
Potatoes	5 700 000 hectares	7 700 000 hectares
Collective farm households	400 000	18 750 000
	1916	1941
Cows	29 000 000	28 000 000
Sheep and goats	96 000 000	92 000 000

N.B. Progress was rapid in industry but slow in agriculture.
1 hectare = $2\frac{1}{2}$ acres.   KW = kilowatt

Health and Education 1928-1941

	1928	1941
Doctors and dentists	70 000	155 000
Hospital beds	247 000	791 000
Death rate per thousand	20·3	18·3
Teachers	349 000	1 237 000
Pupils	11 589 000	35 528 000
Schools	120 000	199 000

During this period, Stalin's aim 'to catch up with and out-distance America' was not reached; but though not all targets of the Plans were hit, the overall achievement was tremendous (see the tables opposite and above). Russia made great strides forward while the industries of Western countries suffered the depression of the 1930s. The contrast was remarkable. The electricity generated in Russia in 1938 was six times the amount in 1928; one hydroelectric dam, the Dnieprostroy dam opened in 1937, produced more electricity than had been available to the whole of Tsarist Russia. Between 1928 and 1938 the annual production of iron and steel increased four-fold. In the Ural mountains the famous steelworks at Magnitogorsk were built. An American engineer described this great venture: 'Tens of thousands of people were enduring the most intense hardships in order to build blast furnaces and many of them did it willingly with boundless enthusiasm which infected me from the day of my arrival.'

The development of transport did not keep pace with the demands of industry. By 1937 there was about half as much railway track again as in 1913, but the amount of traffic had increased five-fold.

Peasants poured into the towns to man the new factories and the number of industrial workers rose from 11½ million to 27 million. These moujiks had no experience of machinery and there were countless accidents and mechanical breakdowns. Some peasants were inclined to beat a faulty machine as they might punish a stubborn mule.

As the American engineer at Magnitogorsk found, the workers were at first enthusiastic about the Five Year Plan. They looked forward to the time when the new industries would produce enough goods for all to lead comfortable lives. Meanwhile they lived in crowded slums flung up around the new factories. They wore old clothes and food was rationed, but their eyes were on the glorious future. For some the vision faded as year followed year and living standards scarcely improved.

Russian newspapers, novels, broadcasts and films all sang the praises of the heroes of the Five Year Plan or criticized those who failed to reach their production targets. The most famous of the star-workers was Alex Stakhanov, a coal miner. In September 1935 Stakhanov dug 102 tonnes of coal in one shift, fourteen times the normal output (although the newspapers did not report the special preparations which had been made to achieve this record). Stakhanov was treated like a hero and all Russian workers were urged to follow his example. Workers who reached outstanding levels of production became known as 'Stakhanovites' and were given more pay and better housing. Sometimes their performance was helped along by finer machinery and materials than were available to ordinary workers. Following the example of a Stakhanovite, greater output was demanded from other workers in his factory. This was unfair and greatly resented; several Stakhanovites were murdered by their workmates. Sometimes production was increased at the expense of quality. For example, there were complaints about sand in cans of fish and trousers with one leg shorter than the other. Strict discipline was enforced in factories: one day's absence could result in dismissal.

By 1938, when the third Five Year Plan began, Russia was one of the world's greatest industrial nations. But war clouds were gathering in Europe and a great testing time for Russia's new industries lay ahead.

Changes in agriculture

When Stalin took over as leader, agriculture was mainly being carried on by peasants working their own plots. Although all land belonged in law to State, the peasants looked on their farms as their own. Stalin feared that backward villages would hold up the progress towards 'Socialism in one country'. Small scale peasant farming was inefficient and did not provide the Government with the large grain exports needed to pay for foreign machinery. Because of the shortage of consumer goods in the shops the moujiks became increasingly reluctant to market their grain. The Five Year Plans called for millions of extra workers to man the new factories; these could only come from the countryside.

To modernize agriculture, the strips of land belonging to individual moujiks were now to be brought together into huge farms called **collectives.** These could be run efficiently with far less labour by using modern machinery. A collective farm or **kolkhoz,** as it was called, often consisted of several villages and covered an average area of 3000 hectares. It was controlled by a committee elected by the peasants although the chairman might be a 'safe' Party member sent in from outside.

The process of forming collective farms began slowly in 1928. It was hoped that moujiks would join together voluntarily, inspired by the example of the few model kolkhozes which had already been established. To encourage this, the peasants in kolkhozes were to pay less taxes than those working their own farms. But this plan of persuasion was a failure; the moujiks stuck stubbornly to their individual plots.

Unless the agricultural revolution went forward, the industrial revolution, which depended upon it, would fail. Stalin decided to use force despite the terrible memories of the bloody struggle between the Government and peasants during the period of War Communism. Stalin saw the kulaks, the rich peasants who had most to lose, as the main enemies of change. He declared, 'In order to squeeze out the kulaks . . . we must break down the resistance of this class in open battle.' Stalin encouraged poor peasants to seize grain stocks belonging to the kulaks and to hand over their farm implements to the collectives. Squads of party workers were sent into the villages to speed up the process but these campaigns often turned into uncontrolled murder and looting. The secret police played their part too. Fundamentally, collectivization was a struggle between the town-based Communists and the majority of the peasants who clung to their old ways.

An eye-witness described the scene in one village: 'A middle-aged peasant, his face black and blue and his clothes ripped, was led off by two secret police. His grief-stricken wife stood outside her home. The woman held a flaming sheaf of grain in her hands. She tossed the burning sheaf on the the thatched roof of the house, which burst into flames. "Infidels! murderers!" the woman was shrieking. "We worked all our lives for our house. You won't have it".'

Many of those who lost their farms were sent to do forced labour in lumbering camps in Siberia. They were not all kulaks but included many poor peasants who had refused to join a kolkhoz.

Stalin's violent campaign resulted in half the peasants joining collective farms by March 1930, but the countryside was torn apart in what amounted to a civil war. Stalin admitted that many poor moujiks had been persecuted and blamed local Communists, whom he described as 'dizzy with success'. Enforced collectivization was halted and the peasants were allowed to withdraw from the kolkhozes. In five months the number of peasants in collective farms fell by two-thirds, far more than Stalin had expected, and once again force was used. There were, however, concessions to the moujiks. Each peasant family on a collective farm was allowed to have its own small plot for spare-time cultivation and they could keep a few animals and some poultry. By 1934 about three-quarters of the peasants' farms had been brought into collectives.

This change was brought about at a tremendous cost. The amount of food produced fell sharply. Rather than hand over their beasts to the collectives, peasants slaughtered them; the number of horses and cattle on Russian farms fell by half between 1929 and 1933. The country once again felt the bleak hand of famine in 1932 and 1933. Despite the shortages, the Government insisted on the peasants supplying as much grain as before to feed the towns. The number who starved to death is unknown, but it probably ran into millions. It was during this period that Stalin's second wife Nadya committed suicide, in November 1932. Apparently she was driven to despair by the suffering of the Russian people. This event is said to have shaken Stalin's confidence and to have brought him to the brink of resignation.

In 1937 practically all the peasants were in kolkhozes; that is, except for some few millions in forced labour camps. The open opposition of the moujiks had been broken, but their hidden resentment remained. Many peasants did as little as possible in the work brigades of the collective farms and saved their energy for tending their own plots. In 1938 although the private plots of land made up only 3 per cent of the area farmed, they contained over half the cattle.

The collective farms did not own machinery, which was provided by

Machine and Tractor Stations. There were only six of these in 1928 but 2400 by 1932. The 'sacred duty' of the kolkhoz was to produce its quota of grain, eggs, etc. for sale to the Government at very low fixed prices. Produce above the quota grown on the collective farm and the harvest of the private plots could be sold for what they would fetch on the open market. These prices were often ten times as high as those given by the Government. By buying food at low prices and selling it at high prices, the Government raised capital to build new factories and to buy machinery from abroad.

Social changes

The success of the Five Year Plans depended on educating the Russian people. Many more schools were built and by 1934 all children went to a Seven Year School which provided education between the ages of seven and fourteen. Education after the age of fourteen laid particular stress on technical subjects which were directly connected with the Five Year Plan. Stalin did not approve of the free-and-easy methods in many schools and discipline was tightened throughout the educational system. Adults were not neglected. In particular the problem of illiteracy was tackled, and 50 million adults learned to read and write between 1920 and 1940.

For people who were unable to work due to illness there were sickness payments, provided they had a good record at work. There were no payments for the unemployed since they were sent straight to another job. In 1932 a generous system of old age pensions began which gave retired people at least half of their former wages.

Many new hospitals and clinics were built. Large numbers of doctors were trained, over half of them women.

The Communist leaders believed that the easy divorces were causing crime among young people brought up in broken families, and in 1936 stricter marriage laws were reintroduced.

Purges

In Lenin's time about a quarter of a million members of the Communist Party were expelled from the organization. They were believed to have joined for personal advantage or thought to be unreliable in some way. As we have seen, Stalin removed Trotsky and his supporters from the Party after Lenin's death. These 'purges', as they are called, were only a glimpse of what lay in the future.

When some Party leaders had demanded sterner punishment of Trotsky in 1929 Stalin had commented: 'You chop off one head today, another tomorrow, still another on the day after. What in the end will be left of the Party?' This constitutes criticism of his own future actions, for in the 1930s Stalin's attitude completely changed. He felt threatened by enemies both inside and outside Russia. In 1933 Hitler, the sworn enemy of Communism, came to power in Germany. Trotsky, who still had many admirers in Russia, continued to challenge Stalin from his exile abroad. This situation brought out the suspicious and ruthless side of Stalin's nature.

On 1 December 1934 Sergei Kirov, the head of the Communist Party in Leningrad, was murdered in his office by a young Party member, probably acting on Stalin's orders. The secret police seized people accused of being involved in the plot. The net widened and in the spring about forty of Stalin's bodyguard were arrested; two were executed and the rest imprisoned.

The purge snowballed to fantastic proportions. When a man was arrested, his friends fell under suspicion; they too were arrested, then their friends, and so the process went on. A young man described the tension: 'My father used to pace up and down the room all night. He could not sleep because he never knew when he would be the next to go. Every day his friends were disappearing.' As Trotsky remarked, 'Stalin is like a man who wants to quench his thirst with salted water.'

The victims of the purge included all the leading Communists who had stood at Lenin's side in 1917. Kamenev, Zinoviev, Rykov (an ex-Prime Minister), devoted Communists who had for years risked death in fighting the Tsar, now fell under the bullets of Stalin's firing squads. Tukhachevsky, Commander in Chief of the Red Army and hero of the Civil War, was executed in 1938. Half the army's officers, including nearly all the generals, followed in his path.

All of those arrested were accused of planning to murder Stalin and of plotting with foreign countries, including Britain. The evidence was invented by the Secret Police. Some of the accused were tried in public; but only those who were sure to confess. Why did brave and honourable men admit to crimes which they had not committed? There were two main reasons. Firstly, torture was used to extract confessions from stubborn prisoners. One man was interrogated without a break for eleven days. During the last four days he was forced to stand and was aroused with cold water or slapping whenever he collapsed. Secondly, many Communists could not bring themselves to break with the Party which they had served for so many years. They saw that it was essential for the Party to hold together while Russia was undergoing the great strain of the economic revolution of the 1930s. Otherwise everything would be lost to the Communists' enemies, both inside and outside Russia. Trotsky himself had once said 'The Party . . . is always right.' Now the Communist Party was Stalin.

Even this brutal chapter of Russian history contained its grain of humour. Some innocent prisoners did not wish to be tortured yet did not know what to confess to; more imaginative fellow-prisoners helped them out. One man claimed that he belonged to an organization which planned to blow the Soviet Union sky high with artificial volcanoes. Another said that he was planning to blow up a mile-long bridge with a vast quantity of arsenic.

Nobody knows how many thousands were executed in the purge before it began to subside in 1939. Huge numbers who escaped death were sent to forced labour camps in northern Russia. Not even the head of the secret police was safe; two holders of this position were executed.

All this time Stalin was building up his image as the saviour of the

Russian nation. In novels he was portrayed as the saintly father watching over his people. According to the press and radio, which obeyed his orders, he was saving Russia from traitors at home and enemies abroad. Huge portraits of Stalin were displayed everywhere. The mention of his name during a speech brought tumultous applause. No one liked to be the first to stop clapping; the secret police might notice. No Tsar in Russian history earned such respect and fear from his people.

By 1940 Stalin felt safe in Russia. All those whom he feared might challenge him had been swept away, and their places had been taken by younger men who owed their promotion to Stalin and on whose loyalty he could depend. Yet there remained one rival alive: Trotsky, living in a fortified house in Mexico. One of Stalin's agents gained Trotsky's friendship and wormed his way into the house. On 20 August 1940, as Trotsky sat writing at his desk, this young man silently approached. He battered in the head of the unsuspecting writer with an ice axe. Blood spattered over the pages of writing. Trotsky never finished his biography of Stalin.

Fig 13 Leon Trotsky, creator of the Red Army.

SUMMARY – Chapter 4

YOUTH AND EARLY CAREER
Stalin (Joseph Djugashvili) was born in Georgia in 1879, the son of a
cobbler. He went to the village school and later to a strictly run priests'
training college. He joined the Communists and was expelled from
college. Stalin produced revolutionary newspapers and organized
strikes. He was imprisoned and exiled several times. After the March
1917 Revolution, he edited the Communist newspaper *Pravda*. When
the Bolsheviks came to power, he became Commisar of Nationalities.
The Bolsheviks first promised to allow the minority races to set up
independent governments but later changed their minds. Stalin led
troops at Tsaritsyn (later Stalingrad) and Petrograd during the Civil
War.

STALIN TAKES OVER
Stalin became General Secretary of the Communist Party in 1922. As
Lenin had realized, he was gradually building up his personal power,
which he used to have Trotsky expelled from the Party and then
deported from Russia in 1929. Trotsky had opposed Stalin's policy of
'Socialism in one country'.

DEVELOPMENT IN INDUSTRY
Stalin believed it was essential to end N.E.P. and to develop Russia's
industries rapidly if she was to survive in a hostile world. The problem
was tackled by a series of Five Year Plans. Not all targets were reached
and not all goods were of satisfactory quality, but production increased
sixfold between 1928 and 1940. Star workers called 'Stakhanovites'
received special privileges. Workers poured into towns from the
countryside, and at first there was great enthusiasm although living
conditions were poor.

CHANGES IN AGRICULTURE
Stalin believed it was essential to modernize agriculture to provide
grain for export and food and labour for Russia's key industries. Strips
of land belonging to individual peasants were combined to form huge
collective farms. This process was resisted by the peasants, particularly
the rich kulaks, who were treated ruthlessly. After a pause in 1930 the

forced collectivization was completed by 1937. The peasants showed their resentment by doing the least possible work on the collective farms and lavishing care on their small private plots. Agricultural production slumped and there was severe famine in 1932-3. Machine and tractor stations provided equipment for collective farms. The Government bought most of the produce from the farms at low fixed prices.

SOCIAL CHANGES

Many more schools were built and all children received full-time education between the ages of seven and fourteen. Higher education was largely of a technical nature. Millions of adults were taught to read and write. Sickness payments and retirement pensions were introduced and medical services developed. The easy divorce laws were dropped.

PURGES

The purges were caused by Stalin's unreasonable fear of traitors within Russia. He believed that Russia had to be united to face foreign dangers, particularly after Hitler came to power. The purge began after the murder of Kirov, head of Leningrad Communist Party, in 1934 and snowballed rapidly. Victims included surviving Communist leaders from revolutionary days and half the army's officers. New men whom Stalin trusted were appointed. The country lived under a reign of terror although Stalin depicted himself as the saviour of Russia. The purge culminated with the murder of Trotsky in 1940.

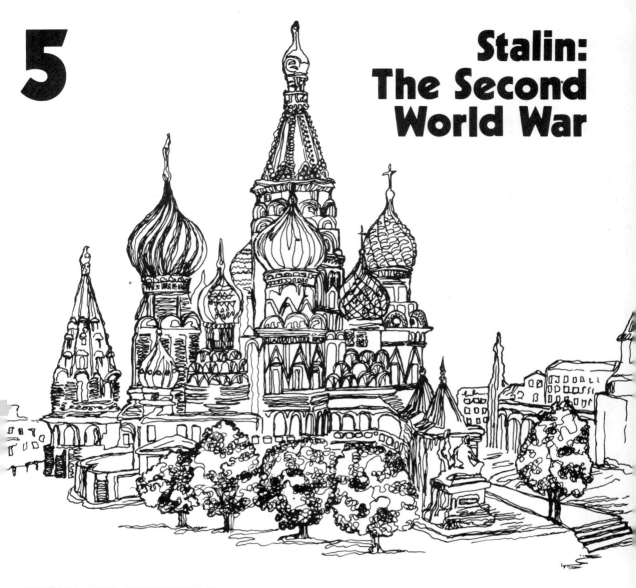

Stalin: The Second World War

5

RUSSIA AND THE WORLD 1924-1933

"We do not want a single foot of foreign territory but we will not surrender a single inch of our territory either." This statement of Stalin's provides the key to his foreign policy for many years. It runs parallel to the aim of 'Socialism in one country'. While Russia was building her industries and changing her system of agriculture she had no energy left over for foreign adventures.

Stalin did not believe that Communist revolutions were likely to occur in any European countries for a long time. While maintaining the special relationship with Germany which had begun with the Treaty of Rapallo, he tried to get on friendly terms with the other governments of Europe. West European countries began to trade with the Soviet

Union. In 1924, France, Britain and Italy sent ambassadors to Russia for the first time since the Revolution. They were still suspicious of Russia but had no wish to drive her deeper into Germany's arms by a hostile attitude.

Stalin controlled foreign Communist parties through the Comintern. If war ever came, their support behind the enemy lines would be valuable to Russia. But the activities of the Comintern sometimes conflicted with Stalin's main aim of establishing friendly relations with other governments.

In 1927 Stalin suffered two setbacks. The British Government was annoyed with the Russians for sending money to help English workers during the General Strike of 1926. In retaliation, they ordered a search of the offices of the Russian Trade Mission in London. They used evidence found there as an excuse to expel all Russian officials from the country. Russian influence suffered a more grievous blow in China. Chiang Kai-shek who came to power on the death of Sun Yat-sen, purged the Communists from his party. Borodin and the other Soviet advisers were sent back home.

Stalin was shaken by these events and made every effort to assure the world of Russia's peaceful intentions. Litvinov, the Russian Foreign Secretary, suggested to a League of Nations conference that all countries should give up all their weapons. This drastic proposal was regarded with deep suspicion and Russia's sincerity was never tested. In 1928 the Soviet Union signed the Kellogg Peace Pact, thereby undertaking not to go to war to carry out her aims.

By 1933 Stalin was in a stronger position. During the previous year, treaties of friendship had been signed with Poland and France. All leading powers, including the U.S.A., now had ambassadors in Moscow. Yet there were clouds on the horizon: in Germany, the first country to offer the hand of friendship to the Soviet Union, Hitler and the Nazi party had come to power.

In the east, the Chinese province of Manchuria was invaded by the Japanese in 1931. This was the first step in an ambitous plan to bring all China under Japanese rule. Stalin did not approve of the conquest but was unwilling to risk war. As a friendly gesture to the Japanese he sold them the Manchurian section of the Trans-Siberian railway at a give-away price, but the Japanese were not impressed and provoked many border clashes. Later in the 1930s this uneasy situation twice flared up into full-scale battles involving hundreds of tanks and planes.

RUSSIA AND THE WORLD 1933-1941

Adolf Hitler, Führer of Germany, hated Communists. In his book *Mein Kampf,* written in prison before he came to power, he marked out the Ukraine and Siberia as areas for future German conquest. Yet Stalin still hoped to continue the special relationship with Germany. He thought that the responsibility of government might change Hitler's ideas.

Although Stalin went out of his way to be friendly towards Hitler, he insured himself against the failure of this policy. In 1934 Russia joined the League of Nations and Litvinov strongly supported the development of the League's peace-keeping activities. Visiting politicians were surprised at the warmth of Russian hospitality. When Anthony Eden, then a junior British Minister, visited Moscow, he was welcomed by Stalin − a rare privilege. At the reception, the Kremlin echoed to the strains of 'God Save the King', a far from revolutionary anthem which had not been heard in Russia since 1917. In 1935 Stalin directed the Comintern to begin the policy of the 'Popular Front'. This meant that Communist parties abroad were to co-operate with other organizations to resist the spread of Nazism. Also in 1935 Russia, France and Czechoslovakia made arrangements to help each other in the event of one them being attacked.

Meanwhile, Hitler's actions became more alarming. In 1936 Germany and Japan made the Anti-Comintern Pact, an agreement to prevent the spread of Communism. Italy, ruled by the dictator Mussolini and his Fascist Party, joined the Pact in 1937. The Spanish Civil War of 1936-1939 gave Hitler a chance to develop the *blitzkrieg* tactics of sudden attack by aircraft and armoured columns which he was to use with devastating success in the Second World War. He supported the eventual victor General Franco against the legal Popular Front government. The latter was aided by Russian supplies despite the fact that the distance involved made this difficult.

In 1938 Hitler began building his empire by taking Austria under his control. The same year he demanded part of Czechoslovakia: German speaking Sudetenland. Britain and France were alarmed at Germany's expansion but reluctant to provoke a war. Finally, after talks with Hitler in Munich, they achieved what the British Prime Minister, Neville Chamberlain, hopefully called 'peace in our time'. Hitler occupied the Sudetenland in exchange for a guarantee that the rest of Czechoslovakia would be left alone. Neither Czechoslovakia itself nor Russia (which had an agreement with France to protect Czechoslovakia) was invited to the Munich talks. Stalin feared that Britain and France had bought off Germany at the Soviet Union's expense; perhaps Czechoslovakia was intended to be Hitler's stepping-stone to the Ukraine. Despite his promise, Hitler occupied the rest of Czechoslovakia in March 1939 and moved a step nearer to plunging Europe into war.

Stalin sought to protect Russia's position by opening talks with both Britain and Germany in the summer of 1939. The British had no confidence in Russia, especially after the recent purges which had weakened the Red Army, and they demonstrated this in the most obvious way: while Chamberlain himself had flown to Germany to talk with Hitler, only a junior official was sent to negotiate with the Russians.

Despairing of coming to an understanding with Britain and France, Stalin drew nearer to Hitler, the arch-enemy of Communism. This suited Hitler, who had decided to attack France. An agreement with

Russia would safeguard his rear. The announcement of the Russo-German treaty in late August astonished the world; the secret of the talks had been well kept. The part of the treaty made public consisted of a promise by both sides not to attack each other but a more sinister section of the treaty had been kept secret. In this, Stalin and Hitler agreed to split Poland between them, Russia regaining the lands of eastern Poland which she had lost by the Treaty of Riga in 1921.

A few days later this agreement came into effect, after the Polish army had been overwhelmed by the German *blitzkrieg* with surprising speed. Britain and France had promised to support Poland if she were attacked and they now declared war on Germany.

Russia remained neutral, but Stalin strengthened his western frontier. In October the Russian army established bases in Estonia, Latvia and Lithuania with the apparent agreement of their peoples. Then Finland was asked to allow the Soviet Union to establish bases on her territory to defend the approaches to Leningrad; Finland refused. Stalin, who in 1917 as Commissar of Nationalities had granted the Finns their independence, now ordered the Red Army to crush them. The Finns made a gallant defence which earned them the admiration of other countries and showed up the weaknesses of the Russian army, but after a struggle lasting four months sheer weight of numbers told, and Finland was forced to cede territory.

During 1940 Stalin watched with surprise the victories of the apparently invincible *Wehrmacht* (German army). Denmark, Norway, Belgium, Holland and France were all hammered to defeat. Hitler had only one failure: the *Luftwaffe* (German air force) was defeated by the R.A.F. in its attempt to seize control of the skies over England. Without air supremacy, Hitler decided to postpone the invasion of Britain. His eyes now turned eastwards, to the Soviet Union. With Russia's grain, minerals and factories at his command, he could strike at Britain with redoubled strength.

The German invasion of Russia

In late 1940 Hitler began to plan 'Operation Barbarossa', the code-name for the invasion of Russia. Stalin appeared to have no suspicion that an attack was near, although in April 1941 he signed a treaty with Japan to safeguard eastern Russia. Winston Churchill, Prime Minister of Britain, sent Stalin a message in April warning him that German forces were building up for an attack on the Soviet Union, but Stalin regarded this as an attempt to trick him into war with Germany. Even when Churchill's warnings were confirmed by Russian intelligence reports, Stalin refused to allow the Red Army to make any preparations that would offend Hitler. He believed that the German troop movements were being misunderstood.

On 22 June 1941, Operation Barbarossa began. At first the Russians did not return the fire of the invading German troops; Stalin still hoped that a local German commander had made a blunder. This illusion was soon shattered as German armoured columns poured into Russian territory.

The two armies were about evenly matched in numbers but the Germans had the advantage of surprise attack and the experience and confidence resulting from their earlier victories. The Wehrmacht planned three main drives: to Leningrad in the north, to Moscow in the centre and to Kiev, capital of the Ukraine, in the south. At first the German troops advanced rapidly along most of the 1600 kilometre front, gaining hundreds of kilometres in a few weeks; but the swift collapse of the Red Army on which Hitler had counted did not occur.

Stalin did not appear in public for almost a fortnight after the invasion started. According to Khruschev, his successor, he was nervous and fearful of the future. If that was so, he had steadied himself by 3 July when, in a broadcast to the Russian people, he expressed his determination to defend the Communist homeland. Stalin said of the German invader, 'He is out to seize our lands . . . to seize our grain and oil. He is out to restore the rule of the landlords, to restore Tsarism . . . The enemy must not be left a single pound of grain or gallon of fuel.' The Russians were to follow a 'scorched earth policy', as in their struggle against Napoleon.

Although industries had been built in central and eastern Russia during the Five Year Plans, most of the Soviet Union's war factories were still in the west. Millions of men and machines were transferred to the east, away from the advancing Germans. This upheaval cut back industrial output by half, although it recovered later, thanks to the tremendous efforts made by the factory workers. When a foreign reporter asked a woman munition worker if she were not tired after working eleven hours a day she replied, 'Our men, the soldiers in the Red Army, fight night and day at the front at forty below zero and they are not tired. How should we *dare* to be tired?'

Stalin made every effort to secure national unity during the war. To strengthen the allegiance of the still large number of Christians in Russia, the persecution of the Church was ended. Church leaders responded by supporting the Government's war efforts. To improve discipline in the army, saluting and the old system of ranks were restored. National groups, like the famous Cossacks, were encouraged to form their own regiments again. Rationing was enforced to make sure that scarce food supplies were distributed fairly among the people.

Winston Churchill once said: 'Nothing that has happened in the West can compare with the wholesale massacres not only of soldiers but of civilians and women and children which have characterised Hitler's invasion of Russia.' By their cruel behaviour the Germans forfeited the support of Russian anti-Communists and consolidated the people behind Stalin. An American who lived in Russia during the war reported the fate of Jews in Minsk: in two days the Germans killed 18 000. They kept them completely without food for three days, then they beat or shot them. But they shot them so carelessly that three-quarters remained alive and when they buried them the whole earth moved.

News of Nazi crimes in the occupied areas reached the soldiers in the front line and the workers in the factories. The people's hatred of the enemy was expressed by Stalin who always ended his speeches with, 'Death to the German invader!' Guerilla bands formed behind the enemy lines; they attacked supply columns and murdered soldiers. In no other country was the whole population more involved in the war effort. Women fought with the infantry, drove tanks and piloted planes. Boys of ten fought with the guerilla bands. There were some Russians whose hatred for Stalin's Communism was so great that they joined the German-backed 'Russian Army of Liberation'. But they were too few to make any real difference.

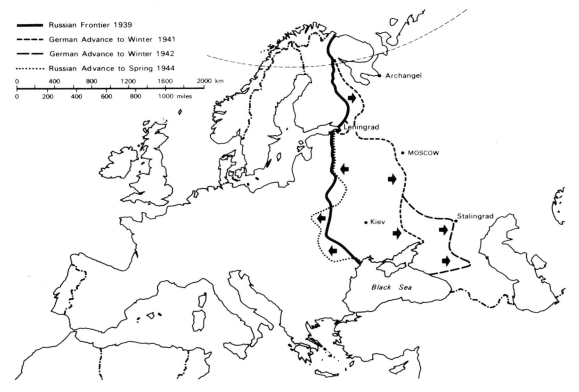

Legend:
- Russian Frontier 1939
- German Advance to Winter 1941
- German Advance to Winter 1942
- Russian Advance to Spring 1944

Scale: 0 400 800 1200 1600 2000 km / 0 200 400 600 800 1000 miles

Archangel · MOSCOW · Leningrad · Kiev · Stalingrad · Black Sea

Map 5 German advance in Russia 1941-1942

Despite all Russia's efforts, by late 1941 the Germans had almost encircled Leningrad, taken Kiev and most of the Ukraine, and advanced within eight kilometres of Moscow. They had captured two million Russian soldiers. In November 1941 Hitler announced joyfully, 'No army in the world can ever recover from such losses, not even the Russians.'

Leningrad was besieged for two and a half years. The population endured bombardment by German artillery and aircraft and the horror of slow starvation. One man described his experiences: 'Food – people ate anything during the famine; it was terrible. They ate glue from the furniture, machine oil – anything. They scratched up the dirt from the bombed place where the food had been stored and made soup . . . All the dogs and cats were gone soon.' Over a million people died during the seige, most of them from starvation, but the city remained defiant and uncaptured.

As the Wehrmacht drew near to Moscow, Government Departments were evacuated and panic seized a section of the population. Stalin himself stayed in the city, and news of this helped to restore confidence. Until May 1941, Stalin held no government post, but contented himself with controlling the country as General Secretary of the Communist Party. He then became Prime Minister, and as Commander-in-Chief of the armed forces he later took the rank of Marshal of the Soviet Army.

Whereas Winston Churchill delighted in visiting the theatres of war and had to be restrained by the King from accompanying the Normandy invasion forces, Stalin directed operations from his office in the Kremlin, with only one visit to a front line area; but one cannot accuse him of cowardice, remembering his dangerous exploits as a revolutionary. The two war leaders were alike in other respects: both showed tremendous energy, often working into the early hours of the morning; both liked to concern themselves with small details as well as planning the overall direction of the war; and both embodied the tenacious spirit of their peoples.

The harsh winter of 1941 saw the German army suffering its first major setback. Over-confidence had resulted in Hitler sending his men to Moscow with only their summer uniforms. Water froze in the radiators of their motor vehicles; there was no anti-freeze. Stalin transferred the brilliant General Zhukov to the Moscow front to launch a vigorous counter-attack. The Germans discovered the superiority of the Russian T34 tanks whose heavy armour withstood the shells of their anti-tank guns. The Wehrmacht was pushed back between eighty and three hundred kilometres and the morale of the Red Army rose.

Fig 14 Red Army soldiers advancing through deep snow behind the cover of a tank.

In the first half of 1942, the Germans moved forward again. This time they struck south in an attempt to capture the rich oil fields of the Caucasus. The Russians fought desperately to hold back the German assault. They asked their allies the British and Americans (America entered the war in December 1941) to open a 'Second Front' against Germany by attacking in the west. The Russians were already receiving massive quantities of food and equipment from their allies. These were carried in convoys to Archangel through waters infested with U-boats and ice-floes, or transported overland through Persia.

The Russians were grateful for this help, but it was not enough. It seemed to them that they were taking the full brunt of the German attack while their allies waited. Stalin feared that they were waiting for Germany and Russia to exhaust each other so that Britain and America could dictate the peace terms. In fact, the same argument could well have applied to Russia in the period 1939-41. Churchill came to Moscow in August 1942 and a flaming row developed when he told Stalin that the Second Front would not be opened that year. The Allies landed in North Africa in November 1942 and in Southern Italy in September 1943 but these operations were on too small a scale to relieve greatly the pressure on the Red Army.

The tide of war turns

Hitler had singled out Stalingrad as the key target of his 1942 offensive. This city stretched for twenty miles along the west bank of the Volga, and control over it would cut off Moscow from the oil fields of the Caucasus. Moreover, the city was the scene of Stalin's triumph during the Civil War and bore his name. Its capture became a question of deep personal importance to Hitler; its defence was of more than military significance to Stalin. Stalingrad became the focus of the entire Russo-German war, the supreme testing-ground.

In mid-September the battle began. Hundreds of aircraft bombed the city; thousands of guns poured their shells into it until the streets were only heaps of rubble. The Russians fought superbly among the ruins of the town and did all that was humanly possible to obey Stalin's order, 'Not a step back!' Hitler himself decided the battle strategy and by early November he was convinced that victory was his. But the Führer's eyes were riveted too closely on the city. From the north and south of Stalingrad, Russian armies were striking out to encircle the German forces, and by 23 November the Germans were trapped in a ring of steel which began relentlessly to close on them. Desperate attempts to break out were beaten off, a relief force was defeated and supply planes were shot out of the sky. On 1 February 1943 the ragged remnants of the German force, led by Marshal Paulus, surrendered. The Wehrmacht had lost over half a million men – most of them killed – and enormous quantities of equipment. Hitler vented his rage on Marshal Paulus because he had surrendered instead of fighting to the death: 'A man like Paulus I cannot understand . . . He could have gone to heroic eternity . . . Instead he chose to go to Moscow.' The victory at Stalingrad was a tremendous inspiration not only to the

Fig 15 (opposite page) Russian soldier at Stalingrad.

66

Fig 16 Stalin,
Roosevelt and
Churchill at the
Tehran
Conference in
1943.

Russians but also to their allies. Coventry, the most bombed city in Britain, presented the Stalingrad Sword to the people of that town.

By February 1943, the Russians had regained nearly all the land lost during the German advance of 1942, and in the summer the Germans mounted their last major offensive without success. The Red Army now had a significant advantage in men and equipment over the Wehrmacht. The long siege of Leningrad was lifted in the spring of 1944. Almost the whole of the Soviet Union was once again in Russian hands.

The Second Front was opened on 6 June 1944. A great Anglo-American invasion fleet left England's south coast to land on the Normandy beaches, and this long-awaited attack in the west was accompanied by a Russian offensive in the east. The Wehrmacht was henceforth to be crushed between the two advancing armies.

In late April 1945, Russian troops reached Berlin and joyfully linked up with American forces. Hitler directed the hopeless last battle from a bunker beneath the city. As the empire which was to have lasted a thousand years crumbled around him, Hitler and his newly married wife committed suicide. The bodies were carefully destroyed to prevent their falling into enemy hands. On 7 May Admiral Doenitz, the new Führer, surrendered to the Allies.

Russia's short, final contribution to Allied victory began on 8 August 1945 when she declared war on Japan. Soviet troops swarmed over the border into Japanese-occupied Manchuria. At midnight on 14th August the Japanese surrendered after the Americans had dropped atomic bombs on the cities of Hiroshima and Nagasaki.

No country contributed more to final Allied victory than Russia. No country on either side suffered more. 70 000 towns and villages lay shattered. Of the five million Russian soldiers taken prisoner, over half had died in German hands. It has been estimated that a total of twenty million Soviet citizens, civilians as well as soldiers, died in the Second World War.

The Russian Communist state had faced the supreme test, and unlike the Tsarist state of the First World War, it had emerged victorious.

SUMMARY – Chapter 5

RUSSIA AND THE WORLD, 1924-1933

Stalin aimed to establish friendly relations with foreign countries while building up Russia's industrial power. The Comintern's activities made it harder to achieve this aim. In 1924, France, Britain and Italy sent ambassadors to the U.S.S.R. There were setbacks to Stalin's policies in 1927, when Soviet officials were expelled from Britain and China. Russia joined the Kellogg Peace Pact and suggested that all countries should disarm. In 1932 the U.S.S.R. signed treaties with Poland and France. The Russians accepted the Japanese occupation of Manchuria in 1931 but there was border fighting later.

RUSSIA AND THE WORLD, 1933-1941

Hitler, who planned the German occupation of Russian lands, came to power in Germany in 1933. Stalin still tried to keep on friendly terms with Germany. In 1934, the U.S.S.R. joined the League of Nations. Germany, Japan and Italy made the anti-Comintern Pact. The Comintern began the policy of the Popular Front. Hitler aided Franco in the Spanish Civil War, while Stalin helped the Republican government.

THE GERMAN INVASION OF RUSSIA

Stalin disregarded reports of German preparation for invasion. In June 1941, German troops invaded and advanced rapidly. Factories were moved eastwards away from the advancing enemy. To secure national unity, Stalin ended the persecution of the Church. Disapproval of German cruelty united the country behind Stalin. Guerilla bands formed behind enemy lines. By late 1941, Hitler's armies had taken most of the Ukraine and were near Moscow. The siege of Leningrad began. The Red Army drove the Wehrmacht back from Moscow, but in 1942 the Germans struck south towards the Caucasus oil fields. The Russians received supplies from the British and Americans, but wanted them to relieve the pressure on the Red Army by opening the 'Second Front' in the west.

THE TIDE OF WAR TURNS

The battle of Stalingrad, which opened in September 1942, marked the turning point of the war. After a bitter struggle, the German forces under Paulus were encircled and forced to surrender. The Russians advanced and by early 1944 had lifted the siege of Leningrad and cleared almost all the U.S.S.R. of Germans. In June 1944, the invasion of France began and Germany was squeezed between the Anglo-American and Russian armies. After Hitler's suicide Germany surrendered, in May 1945. The Soviet Union declared war on Japan shortly before it was defeated. The war had devastated Russian lands and killed twenty million of her people, but the country emerged victorious.

6 Stalin's Last Years

THE ORIGIN OF THE COLD WAR

When Soviet and American troops first met in Germany in April 1945, the Russian major said: 'This is a great day, the meeting of two great nations; we hope this will be the basis for peace in the world.' These words were a reflection of the affection and respect which had grown up between the peoples of the U.S.A. and the U.S.S.R. during the war. Yet even before the fruits of victory had been fully savoured, the wartime unity of Russia and the Allies crumbled as old fears and suspicions came once more to the surface. The Communists remembered the wartime wrangles over the Second Front and how many years earlier the Allies had intervened to help the White Armies. The Western powers recalled that the Communists' ultimate aim was to overthrow Capitalism.

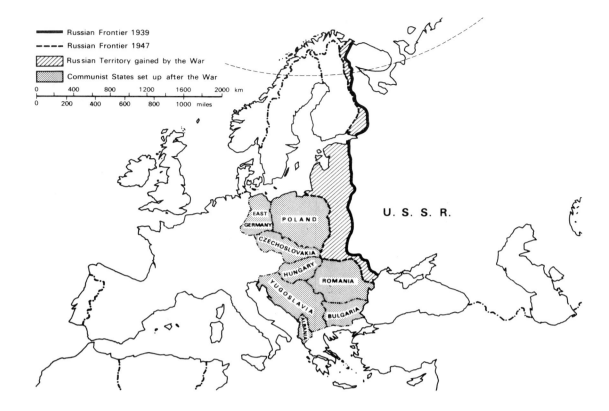

0   400   800   1200   1600   2000 km

0   200   400   600   800   1000 miles

U. S. S. R.

EAST GERMANY

POLAND

CZECHOSLOVAKIA

HUNGARY

ROMANIA

YUGOSLAVIA

ALBANIA

BULGARIA

Map 6 U.S.S.R.'s gains in the West in the Second World War

As a result of the settlements at the end of the war, the U.S.S.R. pushed her frontier well to the west. Altogether, she gained about 51 800 square kilometres, twice the area of the United Kingdom, and 22 million people (see the map above). The largest slice of these gains came from Poland, which had to give up the Western Ukraine. In return, Poland was given part of East Germany up to the Oder-Neisse rivers.

For Stalin, the situation of 1945 was full of dazzling prospects. In their advance to the west, the Red Army had occupied countries in eastern Europe: Poland, East Germany, Czechoslovakia, Hungary, Rumania, Bulgaria, Yugoslavia and Albania. Stalin's first concern was to take from these countries the supplies which were needed to rebuild Russia's industries and to feed her people. Teams of Russian experts were sent to organize this. They organized the transfer of far more goods than Russia's Western Allies expected.

Pro-Russian governments came to power in the countries occupied by the Red Army, largely reflecting Allied wartime agreements. At first Stalin encouraged the East European Communists to work in co-operation with other political parties. Later, when relations with the West deteriorated, the Communists openly took control. Probably only in Albania and Yugoslavia did they have the support of most of the people.

Western countries were afraid that Communism might spread to

Turkey, and to Greece, Italy and France where there were strong Communist parties. Behind this threat they saw the might of the Soviet Army, the largest in the world. To combat this danger President Truman offered in March 1947 aid to any states faced by a Communist take-over. This policy was called the Truman Doctrine.

Russia considered the U.S.A., the greatest Capitalist country, a dangerous rival. While large areas of the U.S.S.R. had been devastated by the war, America had emerged unscathed and economically stronger. Moreover, she alone possessed the most terrifying of modern weapons, the atomic bomb, which President Truman had decided not to share with Russia. Stalin felt that he needed the East European Communist 'satellite' states to strengthen and protect the U.S.S.R.

Thus mutual suspicion and fear poisoned relations between Russia and her former allies after 1945. It prevented the U.S.S.R. joining in the Marshall Plan which the U.S.A. launched in 1947 to restore the economies of war devastated countries. This hostility which stopped short of fighting was called the 'Cold War'.

The United Nations

The *United Nations Organization* was formed at San Francisco in 1945. It was the successor to the League of Nations and its principal task was to prevent war. In the early days of peace, people believed that the great powers would work together in the United Nations to make a better world.

Unfortunately, the United Nations soon became an arena in which the U.S.A. and the U.S.S.R. struggled for the support of the smaller nations. In this contest America was the more successful; but though the U.S.A. controlled more votes, Russia could hold up action by the Security Council – the part of the United Nations responsible for peace-keeping operations – by using her *veto,* the overriding vote possessed by all the great powers in the Security Council. The U.S.S.R. also refused at first to join most of the 'specialized agencies' of the United Nations such as the World Health Organization. Russia saw the United Nations as an instrument which America was using to increase her power. It was another front of the Cold War.

COLD WAR — EVENTS IN EUROPE

In 1947, following the Truman Doctrine, the U.S.S.R. set up the **Cominform (Communist Information Bureau)** as the successor to the Comintern. The main task of this organization was to co-ordinate the activities of the satellite states with those of Russia.

One of these satellites, Yugoslavia, was never firmly under Stalin's control. Its ruler was Marshal Tito, a Communist leader who had commanded partisan armies against the Germans with great success. He resented the role which Stalin had chosen for Yugoslav as wheat producer for the more industrial Communist countries. Tito wished to build up Yugoslav industries and also refused to collectivize the farms as Stalin had wished. Stalin had no doubt about his ability to deal with this defiance. He is reported to have said: 'I will shake my little finger and there will be no more Tito!' Russia forced the Communist group of countries to cut off trade with Tito and waited for Yugoslavia to collapse. Tito, confident in the support of his people, established friendly relations with the Western powers and obtained loans from the World Bank of the United Nations. He survived Stalin's fury.

Tito had shown that a Communist state could exist without Russian support and his example was to be followed later by others. Stalin was alert to the danger, and in a series of bloody purges he removed East European Communist leaders who put national interests before support of Russia. The U.S.S.R. Marshal Rokossovsky was sent to take command of the Polish army. Peasants who resisted collectivization were forcibly suppressed, as had happened earlier in Russia. By 1951 Stalin had stamped out opposition in the satellite countries.

The Communist states built a wall of barbed wire along their frontiers to isolate their peoples from the West. Churchill called this barrier the 'Iron Curtain'.

The growing hostility between Russia and the West was illustrated by events in Germany, which at the end of the war had been divided between Russia, Britain, France and the U.S.A. The Allied Control Commission which was formed to co-ordinate development in the four zones did not work smoothly. The three Western powers worked closely together and their zones became merged into one, and between this Western zone and the Russian one arose the Iron Curtain. The Western area, backed by the economic resources of the U.S.A., recovered more quickly than the Communist zone.

Berlin, as the capital of Germany, was split between the four powers although it lay deep in the Russian zone. It was a gap in the Iron Curtain which enabled hundreds of thousands of East Germans to escape to the more prosperous West. In 1948 Stalin decided to force the Western powers out of Berlin by cutting off all road and rail traffic. The Allies mounted a gigantic airlift to bring in food and supplies to the two million people of West Berlin which continued day and night for eleven months. Stalin, realizing that he could not cut this vital artery without risking a third world war, finally raised the blockade. In 1949 the people of Eastern and Western Germany were each granted a large degree of independence under separate governments. This was a measure of the success in overcoming the bitterness which had divided Germany and her former enemies; but it was also a measure of the failure of the former allies to co-operate in forming one German government.

The *North Atlantic Treaty Organization (N.A.T.O.)* was set up in 1949. This was a defensive alliance dominated by the U.S.A. and including Canada, France and Britain. West Germany later joined the Organization. Russia formed a counter-balance to this in which she joined her armies to those of the Communist satellites of East Europe. Although this agreement, the Warsaw Pact, was not signed until 1955, it only set the seal on arrangements which had been made earlier.

74

Map 7 Events in
Asia

EVENTS IN ASIA

The greatest victory for Communism after the war came in China. Following the defeat of the Japanese, open warfare once again broke out between the Nationalists and Communists. Chiang Kai-shek, the Nationalist leader, had vast quantities of American equipment which he had received for fighting the Japanese. Mao Tse-tung, commander of the dedicated Communists, had the support of most of the peasants, who expected to gain from land reforms. Many of Chiang's men were disloyal and went over to the Communists. After a series of bloody battles, the remnants of the Nationalist armies left the mainland and retreated to the island of Formosa in 1949. Mao became chairman of the People's Republic of China, a country with the largest population in the world: over 600 million. During the struggle, the Chinese Communists had received little Russian aid. Another Communist colossus had emerged to take its place beside the U.S.S.R.

In Vietnam the French, who had ruled the country before the war, tried to reassert their authority after the defeat of the Japanese. The Communist Ho Chi Minh led a native movement backed by Russia which resisted the French. After Mao Tse-tung came to power in nearby China, the Americans sent considerable help to the French in

75

Vietnam. In 1954 the French withdrew, leaving the Americans backing a non-Communist government in South Vietnam, while China and Russia were sending aid to the communists in the North. This bitter war continued on an ever-increasing scale until a precarious peace which gave neither side victory was established in 1973. While the Russians and Chinese were not actively involved in the fighting, 56 000 Americans died and Vietnamese casualties ran into millions.

After the surrender of the Japanese, Russia occupied North Korea and U.S.A. took over the South. They both established governments friendly to themselves and then withdrew. Then in 1950 the North Koreans, apparently encouraged by Stalin, invaded the South. Possibly Stalin anticipated that the war would widen and involve the Western powers and Communist China; Russia could then have waited on the side-lines while her enemies and a potential rival weakened and perhaps destroyed each other. As the North Koreans drove deep into South Korea, the conflict was discussed in the Security Council of the United Nations. The Russian delegates were absent from the meeting, and this allowed the United Nations to take action which the veto of the U.S.S.R. might have prevented.

The U.N. forces came from sixteen nations, including Britain, but they were mainly Americans and were commanded by the American General MacArthur. These forces repelled the invaders and advanced far into North Korea, Chinese 'volunteer' soldiers coming over the border to oppose them. General MacArthur wanted to attack China with atomic bombs, but this would have involved the United States in a major war; MacArthur was dismissed by President Truman and the conflict confined to Korea. Eventually, in 1953, a truce was arranged with the cease-fire line running close to the original frontier. About 3 million Koreans had died in the bloody and inconclusive conflict between North and South Korea.

The Communist parties made armed bids to seize power in Burma and Malaya after the war. In both cases they operated as guerilla bands in the jungles for several years before they were overcome.

Unlike Germany, Japan was not occupied by all the Allies, but only by American troops. Russia, however, gained South Sakhalin and the Kuril Islands from Japan. Stalin resented the growth of American influence in an area close to his own shores and refused to sign the Japanese Peace Treaty of 1951; but after Stalin's death the U.S.S.R. signed a separate peace treaty with Japan, in 1956.

Agriculture after the war

Russian agriculture suffered greatly from the effects of war. As the Germans retreated they left behind them barren battlegrounds. The harvest of 1945 was only 60 per cent of that of 1940. The system of collective farms was breaking down as peasants benefited from the confusion by enlarging their own private plots. Rumours had spread that collective farming would be abandoned after the war, but this was far from Stalin's intention, and land was reclaimed from the peasants and restored to the collectives.

The agricultural situation was worsened by the failure of the 1946 harvest after the worst drought of the century. However, no famine followed as in 1922, for the Government brought in grain from the satellite states and distributed the available food supplies efficiently.

A reorganization scheme was carried through by Nikita Kruschev, then in charge of agriculture, which increased the size of the collective farms and reduced their number from 250 000 to 95 000 by the end of 1952. One of the ideas was to make it easier for the Communist Party to control the farms; there were fewer Party members in the countryside.

Despite the reorganization, results were disappointing. Conditions were so grim on some collective farms that peasants were sent food parcels by relations in prison camps. Taxes were increased on products from private plots, but peasants still lavished care on them to the neglect of the collectives. In 1952 the stock of cattle was below that of 1928 and grain production was low.

Industry after the war

35 000 factories were destroyed in the war and 25 million people were made homeless. Stalin's Plan of National Reconstruction, launched in 1946, was an attempt to repair the ravages of war and to prepare for the dangers which he saw looming ahead. Above all, military equipment had to be produced to maintain the strength of the armed forces. German scientists were brought in to help the Russian research in atomic weapons and rocketry. This work bore important fruit, in the development of the atomic bomb in 1949.

Newly constructed heavy industries in central and eastern Russia had proved vital in the war, and now the main programmes of development were carried out in these regions. Machinery confiscated from Germany was set to work in Russian factories. German-built locomotives were operated on Russian railways as the transport system was reconstructed. But the principal reason for progress was Russia's own industrial development. By 1948 the U.S.S.R.'s factories were producing as much as in 1940. In 1952, near the end of Stalin's life, industrial production was twice the pre-war total. This was a tremendous achievement.

Because Russian industry was harnessed to military needs, consumer goods were still in short supply in 1952. Good clothes and luxury goods were scarce, although more were appearing in the shop windows. More serious was the continued shortage of housing. Life was still hard for the ordinary people, but there was a slow and definite improvement.

STALIN'S DICTATORSHIP

In the years after the war Stalin aged visibly, but though his face became thin and lined, his mind remained alert and obstinate. He kept all power in his own hands, not even calling a Congress of the Communist Party.

Stalin continually emphasized the danger of attack by the U.S.A. in

the miserable conditions of post-war Russia, he encouraged his people
by pretending that life was even worse in the West. The Iron Curtain
around the U.S.S.R. which isolated her from the West helped Stalin's
propaganda. At the same time Stalin began to rewrite the history of the
war, discrediting the efforts of his former allies and making Russia
seem solely responsible for Germany's defeat. He even claimed the
credit for the victory over Japan, although Russia had only joined the
war a week before Japan's surrender.

The anti-American campaign in the U.S.S.R. was paralleled by a
persecution of suspected Communists in the U.S.A. This was led by the
fanatical Senator McCarthy, who blighted the lives of many innocent
people before he was finally discredited.

Now that national unity was no longer ensured by common hatred of
the invader, Stalin's old suspicions emerged. He saw the generals who
had become famous in the war as potential rivals. In retelling the story
of the war, Stalin magnified his own contribution and played down
their efforts. He spread the story that Marshal Zhukov was governed by
superstition: this hero of the defence of Moscow and the capture of
Berlin was said to have picked up a handful of earth to smell it before
deciding whether to launch an attack. The film *The Fall of Berlin*
presented Stalin as solely responsible for Russia's victory. Zhukov was
sent off to an obscure post in the east.

Not only generals but scientists, writers and artists were made to feel
the weight of Stalin's authority. Their work was governed by what
Stalin considered suitable and he was the supreme expert in all
matters. He supported the scientist Lisenko in a dispute over a genetic
theory and even entered into a discussion on Russian grammar.

Some national groups who had co-operated with the Germans, such
as the Crimean Tartars, were deported from their lands and sent to
prison camps. They often put up a fierce — but vain – resistance.
Sometimes even returning prisoners were clapped in jail, for disobeying
Stalin's order not to surrender to the Germans.

Late in 1952 came what appeared to be the first instalment of a new
purge. Nine doctors, seven of them Jews, were accused of murdering
Zhdanov and of conspiring to kill military leaders. Zhdanov, a senior
Communist Party official, who had died in 1948, was widely believed to
have been Stalin's choice as his successor. According to Khruschev,
Stalin told the Minister of Security, 'If you do not obtain confessions
from the doctors we will shorten you by a head.' Not surprisingly,
confessions were forthcoming, after the use of torture.

On 4 March 1953 came the news that Stalin had suffered a stroke. He
died the next day. People were dumbstruck; after twenty-five years
they could not imagine a Russia without Stalin.

The body was preserved and laid beside that of Lenin in the
Mausoleum in Red Square. Stalin's death came just in time for leading
Communists who were in danger of being involved in the doctor's
purge. The rumour spread that Stalin had been poisoned, but this has
since been denied by his daughter Svetlana, now living in the U.S.A.,
who was present at his deathbed.

Stalin's achievements

Under Stalin Russia had been transformed. Education and health services had vastly expanded; industry employed three times as many people as before. A great war had been won and the resultant devastation gradually overcome. Communist governments had been set up in the countries of Eastern Europe. On the negative side, the collectivization of farms had caused great human misery without creating an efficient system of agriculture, and the people of Russia had been cowed by the activities of the Secret Police.

Like Peter the Great, Stalin, caring nothing for suffering, had seized Russia by the neck and heaved her into the forefront of the world's nations.

The life of Stalin

A SUMMARY (Joseph Djugashvili)

1879	Born in Georgie, son of a cobbler.
1899	Expelled from priests' training college for revolutionary views.
1902-17	Joined the Bolsheviks, and was imprisoned and exiled several times for revolutionary activities.
1905	His first wife died after a year's marriage.
1917	Took part in the Bolshevik Revolution and became Commissar of Nationalities.
1919	Married for the second time.
1918-21	Played an important part in the Civil War.
1922	Became General Secretary of the Communist Party.
1924-29	After Lenin's death, began to take over the leadership, defeating Trotsky and his supporters, who opposed Stalin's policy of 'Socialism in one Country'.
1928-41	Five Year Plans accelerated Russia's industrialization concentrating on heavy industry at the expense of consumer goods.
1928-37	Collectivized Russia's agriculture causing famine and great suffering without making farming efficient.
1932	Suicide of his wife Nadya.
1934-39	Removed rivals and those suspected of disloyalty in the great purge.
1939	Made agreement with Hitler for the occupation of Poland.
1941-45	Became Prime Minister and led the Russian forces to victory against Germany.
1945-48	Established the Communist satellite states of Eastern Europe.
1945-53	Organised post-war reconstruction. Continued his strict rule of the Russian people behind the Iron Curtain.
1953	Died after two strokes.

THE ORIGIN OF THE COLD WAR

After victory, the war-time unity of Russia and her allies disappeared. As a result of the war, the U.S.S.R. had gained a large area of land, mainly from Poland. Communist governments were set up in the East European countries occupied by the Russians. Western countries feared that the Red Army might be used to extend Communism further still. In turn, Stalin felt threatened by the U.S.A., which had developed the atomic bomb. The East European satellite states gave him a protective belt of territory.

THE UNITED NATIONS ORGANIZATION

The U.N. was formed in 1945 to prevent future wars, but it became the scene of a tussle between the U.S.S.R. and the U.S.A. for the support of the smaller nations. In this, the U.S.A. had more success, but the U.S.S.R. used its veto in the Security Council to counter American influence.

THE COLD WAR – EVENTS IN EUROPE

The Cominform was set up in 1947 to replace the Comintern. Yugoslavia, led by Tito, broke away from Stalin's control and survived with help from the West. Stalin purged other East European leaders who sought to free their countries from Soviet domination. The Iron Curtain was built to separate Communist Europe from the West. The Russians blockaded West Berlin for eleven months. In 1949 separate German governments were set up in East and West Germany. The North Atlantic Treaty Organization, led by the U.S.A., was established by the Western powers as a defensive alliance. The East European Communist states made the Warsaw Pact.

THE COLD WAR – EVENTS IN ASIA

In 1949 Chinese Communists, led by Mao Tse-tung, defeated the Nationalist army, commanded by Chiang Kai-shek and supported by the U.S.A. In Vietnam the Communists, led by Ho Chi Minh, prevented the French from regaining control. The Americans became the chief supporters of the non-Communist government of South Vietnam. Ho Chi Minh held the North with aid from China and Russia.

In 1950 the North Koreans, supported by China and Russia, invaded South Korea. A U.N. force, mainly American, drove the North Koreans back and the Chinese intervened. A cease-fire was signed in 1953. Communist guerillas made unsuccessful attempts to seize control in Burma and Malaya.

AGRICULTURE AFTER THE WAR

Much Russian agricultural land was devastated by the war. Peasants had enlarged their private plots at the expense of the collective farms. This land was reclaimed and the collectives reorganized. Recovery was slow.

INDUSTRY AFTER THE WAR

Many factories were destroyed in the war and 25 million people were made homeless. Stalin concentrated on building up heavy industry to boost Russia's military power. By 1952 industrial production was double the pre-war total, but houses and consumer goods were in short supply.

STALIN'S DICTATORSHIP

Stalin kept power in his own hands. All aspects of life came under his strict control. He criticized the conduct of the West in the war and claimed that post-war conditions there were worse than in Russia. National groups accused of war-time disloyalty were punished. In 1952 a new purge began, but before it could develop Stalin died of a stroke.

7 Khruschev

STALIN'S SUCCESSORS

THE panic that swept through Moscow at the news of Stalin's death worried the Communist Party leaders. To gain the support of the people they began to relax the iron grip in which Stalin had held the country. Some prisoners were released, including seven of the nine doctors (presumably the other two had died in prison). More consumer goods were promised, and the quotas to be produced by collective farms for sale to the government were reduced.

After Stalin died, George Malenkov became Prime Minister and General Secretary of the Communist Party. It was clear that he had not inherited Stalin's position, but was only the foremost of a group of leaders. These included Beria, the Chief of Police; Molotov, the Foreign Secretary; and Zhukov, the Army leader.

On the edge of this group of prominent leaders was Nikita Khruschev, who had controlled agriculture in Stalin's last years. Khruschev came to the fore when, after a few days, he replaced Malenkov as General Secretary of the Communist Party.

The first open breach in the new leadership came with the arrest of Beria in the summer of 1953. As Chief of Police, he had been responsible for enforcing Stalin's dictatorship, and was the most hated man in Russia; his downfall was a way of ensuring the popularity of the new leaders. Beria, who had brought baseless charges against so many others, was now himself accused of an incredible crime: he was charged with having been a British secret agent for thirty years. More credible was the accusation of 'evil scheming to gain power'. He was shot after a secret trial.

Although the remaining leaders preserved the appearance of unity, a struggle for power went on behind the scenes. In this Khruschev used his influence as General Secretary to promote his supporters to positions of influence within the Party. Stalin before him had prepared his own path to power in this way.

In February 1955, Malenkov resigned as Prime Minister, confessing that he was too inexperienced for such responsibility. His resignation was associated with his policy of providing more consumer goods at the expense of heavy industry and the army. He was replaced by Nicholas Bulganin. Under Stalin, Malenkov would have been imprisoned or executed. Now he was merely demoted to a less important post: Minister of Electric Power Stations. This event set the pattern for the milder character of the new regime. Khruschev said in 1955, 'Stalin was a god; he could make and unmake men and things; we can't.'

The period of joint leadership lasted for four years. In 1957 an attempt was made to oust Khruschev from the group of leaders. Khruschev turned the tables on his opponents by calling a meeting of the Central Committee of the Communist Party. One of Khruschev's friends spoke for six hours while his supporters were flown to the meeting from distant provinces. The Central Committee found Molotov and Malenkov guilty of working against the interests of the Communist Party. Molotov, once Foreign Secretary, was sent as ambassador to Outer Mongolia. Ex-Prime Minister Malenkov found himself managing a Siberian power station.

Late in 1957 Marshal Zhukov, Minister of Defence, was removed for seeking to increase military influence at the expense of the Party. In January 1958 Bulganin resigned as Prime Minister. Later he confessed to plotting with the so-called anti-Party group. Bulganin was replaced by Khruschev. Khruschev now held both of Stalin's old posts and was clearly his successor as far as it was possible for one man to be.

KHRUSCHEV'S EARLIER LIFE

Khruschev, who was born in 1894 in South Russia, once vividly described to foreign visitors his family background and early life.

'My grandfather was a serf, the property of a landlord who could sell him if he wished or trade him for a hunting dog. He could neither read nor write and he had a hard life. He had a bath twice in all his years: once when he was christened as a baby, again when the neighbours prepared him for his burial . . . My father was a farmer who worked in the mines in the winter. I was born in Kalinovka, a farming village so poor that only one man in it was able to own a pair of boots . . . I began working as soon as I could walk. I herded the calves, the sheep.'

Khruschev had little schooling. He could not read or write properly until his twenties, when he went to evening classes.

At the age of fifteen, Khruschev went to work in the coalmines of the Donbas. 'There I discovered something about Capitalists. All they wanted from me was the most work for the least money that would keep me alive. So I became a Communist.'

Later, while working in a factory, he organized a collection for the relatives of strikers who had been shot in the Lena goldfields. After this his passport was marked with a special symbol showing that he was a revolutionary.

Khruschev joined the Bolsheviks in 1918 and fought for them during the Civil War. His knowledge of the Donbas mines enabled him to elude White armies by disappearing down a mineshaft, to reappear at the surface miles away. This period was one of personal tragedy for him, as his young wife starved to death during the great famine of 1922.

After the Civil War, Khruschev was marked out as an intelligent and energetic Party member ripe for promotion. He received special training and began to climb in the ranks of the Communist Party. By 1935 he held the key post of Secretary of the Moscow Communist Party. Khruschev was responsible for purging the Moscow Party of suspected anti-Stalinists.

Fig 17 Moscow Metro: Komsomolskaya Station.

One of his main tasks in the 1930s was to organize the rapid building of the great Moscow *Metro* (underground railway). This was intended as a symbol to the world of the quality and efficiency of Russian Communism. Much of the work was done by prisoners, and it was forced along with little regard for danger. One political prisoner wrote, 'It is a monument not only to Soviet engineering but also to the slave labour that went into its construction.'

In 1939 Khruschev was made a member of the **Politburo,** the top group of Party members who carried out Stalin's plans. He was now at the head of both the Party and the government in the Ukraine; the ruler, under Stalin, of 40 million people. During the war Khruschev had widespread responsibilities. As overlord of the Ukraine it was his task to take over the adjoining area of Poland which Russia gained by the 1939 agreement with Hitler. Then, after the devastating German attack of 1941 and the occupation of the Ukraine, Khruschev organized guerilla warfare. He was later responsible for visiting the front line as the chief Communist Party representative to boost the morale of the troops and to check on the loyalty of the generals.

After the war, Khruschev once again became the Stalin of the Ukraine. Besides the colossal work of reconstruction, he had to deal with local anti-Communist movements which had taken root during the war. He also had to again organize the absorption of the new Polish lands into the U.S.S.R. When these difficult tasks had been achieved he was recalled to Moscow in 1949 to take charge of agriculture. As already mentioned, he was responsible for the amalgamation of collective farms. Khruschev also conceived a highly ambitious plan for abandoning the age-old villages and settling the peasants in 'agro-towns'. There they would lead a modern town life and be transported each day to the fields in lorries. Apart from a few pitiful experiments which failed through lack of resources, this idea did not get off the ground. But though he failed to revitalize Russian agriculture, the task which had defeated everyone since the Revolution, Khruschev retained Stalin's confidence.

We have already traced the process which made Khruschev the most powerful of Russia's leaders by 1958. In that year he was sixty-four years old: a short, plump, bald man with small twinkling eyes. He liked to be the centre of attention and in the past had been criticized for indiscreet behaviour after heavy drinking at parties. Good humoured but at times aggressive, he had little use for the Christian concept of brotherly forgiveness. 'If anyone hit me on the left cheek,' he once said, 'I would hit him on the right one so hard that it would knock his head off.'

De-Stalinization

The relaxation of Government control which followed Stalin's death implied some criticism of the way in which the old dictator had ruled the country. De-Stalinization was carried to an extreme which few imagined possible.

In 1956 at the 20th Communist Party Congress, Khruschev delivered a marathon speech lasting six hours. Much of this speech was a direct attack on Stalin, who for so long had been held up before the Russians as a god; and though it was made in a secret session and was never officially published, it was read out at meetings of the Communist Party all over the country. A full copy of the speech came into the hands of the American Government. Its authenticity was not questioned by Khruschev, and it was confirmed by later events.

In Khruschev's speech Lenin's 'last testament', his dying plea to the Party to replace Stalin, was first made generally known. Khruschev accused Stalin of following the 'cult of the individual' meaning that Stalin built up his image as a superman. Stalin had 'trampled on the principle of collective party leadership'; this principle was now to be restored. Khruschev spoke of the years of terror before the war: 'Mass arrests and deportations of many thousands of people, executions without trial and without normal investigation, created conditions of insecurity, fear and even desperation.' He blamed Stalin for weakening the Red Army by his purges, and for the defeats suffered in 1941. Stalin, he said, had had no idea of the true state of Soviet agriculture, and had not even visited a village after 1928.

Although Khruschev bitterly criticized Stalin for his reckless behaviour in his later years, he did not completely blacken his reputation. In particular the defeat of Trotsky, the development of industry and the decision to collectivize farming were held to his credit. 'In the past,' said Khruschev, 'Stalin doubtlessly performed great services to the Party.'

One may recall that Khruschev himself was in a position of authority at the time of Stalin's purges. In a speech in 1937, Khruschev said, 'Stalin is our hope, he is the light which guides all progressive humanity. Stalin is our banner. Stalin is our victory.' In his speech of 1956, Khruschev excused himself and his colleagues in the following words: 'Attempts to oppose (Stalin's) groundless suspicions and charges resulted in the opponent falling victim to the repression.' The 'repression' was of course Beria and the secret police.

This famous speech was the second which Khruschev made to the 20th Party Conference. In the earlier one he had spoken hopefully of a friendlier relationship with the West. He said that it was possible for Capitalist countries to change peacefully to Communism without a bloody revolution. He also stated that a war between Capitalist and Communist countries was no longer inevitable in these days of nuclear weapons. This was the basis for his policy of 'peaceful co-existence.'

There was a link between Khruschev's two speeches. In overthrowing Stalin from his pedestal, Khruschev made it easier for the Government to follow a more flexible policy in foreign affairs and at home. There was widespread joy as news of Khruschev's speech spread through Russia, although there were riots in Stalin's native Georgia. Thousands of people who had been imprisoned by Stalin were by now released. For some like Marshal Tukhachevsky, executed before the war, it was far too late; but they had their reputations publicly restored.

Under the new leaders, the secret police had much less control over the everyday life of the people. Visitors were once again welcomed into Russia. One Englishman wrote: 'Russians have stopped being afraid of each other. This is the big thing.' He over-estimated the extent of the changes, but the average Russian had certainly become more hopeful and relaxed.

Besides the ordinary tourists, there was a 'cultural exchange' of actors, musicians and other artists between the U.S.S.R. and the West. British audiences started to look forward to visits by the Bolshoi Ballet, Russian musicians and circuses, while British artists like Margot Fonteyn and Laurence Olivier began to number thousands of Russians amongst their admirers. Not only artists but scientists, engineers and salesmen from the Communist and non-Communist countries began to make contact with each other. Although the Iron Curtain had not been demolished, some sizeable gaps had been made in it, and a period known as the 'thaw' began.

The effect of the easing of Communist Party control on writers was particularly striking. Under Stalin's rule their main task had been to glorify both their leader and the nation's economic achievements. Criticism of the Government and its policies was not permitted. Russian literature, which had been raised to a high pinnacle by authors like Leo Tolstoy, had been largely suffocated by the controls. Now the floodgates were opened and Russian authors expressed their new freedom in a spate of works which were often highly critical of Communism.

Among the most famous of these was *Not by Bread Alone* by Vladimir Dudintsev, which described the sufferings of an idealistic inventor in a corrupt society (i.e. present-day Russia).

Khruschev and the other leaders had never intended that criticism should be carried to extremes and from time to time endeavoured to put a brake on the process. In 1958 Khruschev called a group of Moscow writers to his country villa. In the course of the conversation he referred to the Hungarian revolution of 1956 (described later). He ventured the opinion that the trouble was stirred up by writers who had been allowed too much freedom and should have been shot as an example. The implication was only too obvious. One woman writer whom Khruschev had mentioned by name fainted and had to be carried out. But despite these strong words there were no shootings. Nevertheless, the Government clamped down on authors, and in 1958 Boris Pasternak was prevented from accepting the Nobel Prize for Literature for his novel *Doctor Zhivago,* which had been banned in the U.S.S.R.

Despite setbacks, the process of de-Stalinization was carried to its conclusion in 1961. Khruschev then made a further speech attacking Stalin, this time in public. Statues of Stalin were removed, streets renamed and the great town closely associated with Stalin's life, Stalingrad, became Volgograd. Stalin's body was removed from its honoured place in the mausoleum beside Lenin and buried in a plain grave against the Kremlin's walls.

The Soviet Union successfully tested the hydrogen bomb in August 1953 to bring her armoury of weapons to the level of that of the U.S.A. In 1957 she developed the I.C.B.M. (Inter-Continental Ballistic Missile). Khruschev claimed that it was now possible to launch a rocket to any region of the globe. With the development of nuclear weapons, the Russians deemed it prudent to reduce the size of their army from $5\frac{1}{2}$ million in 1955 to $3\frac{1}{2}$ million in 1958.

Khruschev followed a policy of peaceful co-existence with the West. This implied a thaw in the Cold War, but as events showed this was an uneven and uncertain process.

Unlike Stalin, Khruschev enjoyed travelling and visited the West in the more relaxed periods of peaceful co-existence. In July 1955, the leaders of France, Britain, the U.S.A. and U.S.S.R. met at Geneva for the first full-scale 'Summit' Conference for ten years. They were unable to agree on a scheme of disarmament. The mutual suspicion of Communists and non-Communists prevented any acceptable system of weapon inspection being found. No progress was made on the reunification of Germany but, on the other hand, plans were made for closer economic and cultural relations.

In May 1956 'B and K', as Bulganin and Khruschev were popularly known during their period of joint leadership, visited Britain. Khruschev was especially impressed by the behaviour of the passers-by he encountered. He believed that they had been specially chosen for the occasion.

Khruschev went to the U.S.A. in September 1959 at President Eisenhower's invitation. Before he left he made a speech emphasising the importance of peaceful relations between the two super-powers: 'If other countries fight among themselves they can be parted but if war breaks out between America and our country no-one will be able to stop it. It will be a catastrophe on a colossal scale.' During the course of his visit Khruschev made a vivid impression on ordinary people with his friendly down-to-earth manner and his knowledge of farming techniques. He, in turn, was impressed by American agriculture, was lavish in his praise of American skill at sausage-making but insisted on the basic superiority of the Soviet economic system. The visit paved the way for a summit meeting between Khruschev and the Western leaders in Paris in 1960.

On 1 May 1960, Gary Powers, the pilot of a high flying U2 American spying aircraft, was forced down over Russia. This event poisoned the atmosphere before the Paris Conference. Eisenhower refused to apologize for the U2 incident although he promised that no more flights would take place. Khruschev was convinced that America did not want Russia's friendship and left Paris in a fury. The Cold War entered a chillier phase.

On 22 October 1962, President Kennedy announced that U.S. reconnaissance aircraft had photographed missile sites established by the Russians in Cuba. The rockets there might have been for use in a nuclear attack on Washington or New York. Kennedy refused to regard them as the purely defensive weapons the Russians claimed them to be, and blockaded Cuba to prevent military supplies reaching the island. At the same time Kennedy called on Khruschev to dismantle the rocket sites and to ship the equipment back to Russia. Khruschev countered by asking the Americans to remove their rocket bases in Turkey.

As Russian vessels carrying weapons neared Cuba, tension reached breaking point. The world seemed to be on the brink of nuclear war. At the last moment the Russian ships turned round. U Thant, the United Nations Secretary General, was active behind the scenes in persuading the two leaders to come to terms. On 28 October, Khruschev announced that the missiles were being dismantled. Kennedy congratulated him on an act of statesmanship promising that the U.S.A. would not invade Cuba. Khruschev commented: 'They talk about who won and who lost. Human reason won. Mankind won.'

In the mutual relief of having escaped from a terrible disaster, a friendlier spirit pervaded the relations between the two powers. A direct telephone line was opened between the Kremlin and the White House; this 'hot line' would enable the two leaders to communicate personally in the event of any future crisis.

The spirit of conciliation brought an important gain: the Test Ban Treaty of 1963, made between Russia, U.S.A. and Britain. This prohibited any nuclear tests which would contaminate the atmosphere with radio-active dust and so was an important step in safeguarding world health.

The two powers continued to give financial and economic aid to under-developed countries. Egypt, Burma, Ceylon, India and Indonesia received Russian assistance. It has been estimated that Russia spent two billion dollars in this way between 1954 and 1957. Although this was far less than America spent, it was at least as effective in gaining the goodwill of the receiving countries.

Russia still could not agree with the other occupying powers on a way of uniting East and West Germany. Khruschev could not accept a solution which allowed free elections, as this would almost certainly have resulted in the whole of Germany joining with the Western powers. The war was still too fresh in Russian minds for them to contemplate a united, re-armed and unfriendly Germany.

In 1955, East Germany and West Germany became independent countries. West Germany entered N.A.T.O. and began to re-arm. In 1961 the Communist authorities built the Berlin Wall to prevent people from the Eastern sector fleeing to the West. Much bitterness was aroused by this move and by the subsequent shooting of East Germans trying to escape over the wall. Germany continued to be a thorn in the side of world peace.

Foreign Relations – Other Communist Countries

The peoples of Eastern Europe, reluctant members of Stalin's empire, stirred hopefully on his death. In June 1953 there was a rising in East Germany which was crushed by Russian troops. Despite this show of force, the new leaders began to relax Russia's grip on East Europe. The Cominform, Russia's instrument for controlling the satellite states was abolished in 1956. This was part of the process of de-Stalinization.

In his speech to the 20th Party Congress, Khruschev had emphasized that the blame for the quarrel with Yugoslavia lay with Stalin. 'B and K' visited Belgrade and a friendship treaty was signed. Despite this, Yugoslavia never fully returned to the fold, and the Yugoslav Communist Party's individual approach to Communism led to further disagreements in 1958.

Khruschev's 1956 speech was received with delight by many of the Poles, who had become restless under Stalin's heavy yoke. In June 1956, following a rising by workers in Poznan, Gomulka was elected General Secretary of the Polish Communist Party. Gomulka had been sent to prison in 1948 as a supporter of Tito. He relaxed Party control over the population and adopted a more independent line towards the Soviet Union. Gomulka also secured Russian agreement to withdraw Marshal Rokossovsky and his Soviet soldiers.

In Hungary there were student demonstrations inspired by events in Poland. The secret police fired on the demonstrators but many soldiers went over to their side. Imre Nagy, a moderate Communist, came to power and under pressure from the rebels adopted a policy which would have taken Hungary right outside the Communist camp. The U.S.S.R. which had accepted a milder form of Communism in Poland was not prepared to see the complete extinction of Communism in Hungary. Russian tanks rumbled into Budapest. The rebels resisted valiantly but were crushed by superior force. Thousands of them died in the fighting; hundreds of thousands fled abroad as refugees

The U.S.S.R.'s action in Hungary shocked the rest of the world, which saw the re-emergence of the cruel hand of Stalinism. Russia's action came at a time of disunity among the Western powers, for the U.S.A. was in dismay at the Anglo-French invasion of Egypt. In the circumstances, the Western countries found it hard to point an accusing finger at Russia. The United Nations passed a resolution condemning the U.S.S.R. but took no action.

The unfortunate Nagy was tricked into leaving the Yugoslav Embassy where he had sought refuge. It was later announced that he had been executed by the new government headed by Kadar, a pro-Russian Communist. The Hungarian rebels had not lost their cause as completely as first appeared. Having stamped out all opposition, Kadar gradually relaxed some controls over the population.

For Russia, the emergence of China as a communist neighbour with a population over three times her own was a mixed blessing. The U.S.S.R. gave considerable technical assistance to Mao Tse-tung in the first few years. For their part, the Chinese supported Stalin and Russian Communism.

Khruschev's accession to power altered things. The improvement in the relationship between America and Russia was accompanied by a growing hostility between Russia and China. The Chinese continued to believe in the violent overthrow of Capitalism and despised Khruschev for his 'soft' attitude towards the Americans. They resented the

Russians' failure to disclose the secrets of their nuclear weapons to them. Mao Tse-tung refused to sign the Test Ban Treaty when Chinese scientists developed the atomic bomb. The U.S.S.R. supported India when she was involved in a border war with China in 1962.

The Western world looked on with amazement as bitter insults usually reserved for Capitalist targets were hurled between the Communist rivals. Small incidents were magnified out of all proportion; at one time a major political row grew out of a Russian complaint that Chinese students had behaved like cattle in fouling the platform of a Soviet border station. The old national enmity of Russia and China had overwhelmed the unifying influence of Communism.

This rift between China and Russia, although it weakened the Communist group, had its drawbacks for the West. In the earlier period the Russians exercised a restraining influence on the Chinese, once persuading them to abandon a plan for invading Formosa. In the quarrel between the Communist giants most of the satellite states supported Russia, but Albania, which had been horrified by Khruschev's criticism of Stalin, came out on China's side. The general result of this rift was to loosen further Russia's grip on the East European states which formed Stalin's post-war empire. Their peoples had greater freedom and their economic development was no longer subject to such close control as that which Stalin had sought to impose.

In Asian and African countries, Russia and China competed for influence, supplying arms and building railways and harbours.

United Nations

After Stalin's death, the U.S.S.R. began to participate more actively in the work of the United Nations. It joined a number of the specialized agencies, including the World Health Organization, in 1955.

Nevertheless, Khruschev resented the influence of America in the General Assembly. Any Russian attempt to solve a quarrel through the United Nations was like 'putting your head on the chopping block', he said. Russia refused to contribute towards the peace-keeping activities of the United Nations in the Congo and in other areas. Khruschev regarded this rather like acting as paymaster for his enemies' troops. As Russia's relations with the U.S.A. worsened during 1960, Khruschev's hostility towards the United nations increased. He accused Dag Hammarskjold, the highly respected United Nations Secretary General, of acting unfairly towards Communist members. In a famous incident, Khruschev expressed his disagreement with a speech made by Harold MacMillan, the British Prime Minister, by removing his shoe and hammering violently on a desk!

Agriculture

A peasant by birth, Khruschev always showed a strong personal interest in farming. His career as an international statesman did not prevent his spending hours explaining to groups of Russian peasants exactly how to plant potatoes. Khruschev's speeches on agriculture fill eight volumes.

After Stalin's death Khruschev stressed the miserable inefficiency of many Russian farms. There had been nine million more cattle in 1928 than in 1953. One of the reasons why the collective farmers had made little effort to increase production was the low prices paid by the Government; these had often been less than the cost of production. Khruschev made great increases in the Government payments, although more work days were expected from the peasants. By 1958, collective farms were earning three times as much as in 1952. In addition, taxes and restrictions on the sale of goods from private plots were reduced. This all amounted to a new deal for the under-privileged farmworkers. In 1958 the Machine Tractor Stations were closed and their mechanised equipment passed into the ownership of the kolkhozes (collectives).

In 1954 Khruschev announced a stupendous scheme for the expansion of agriculture. This was the Virgin Lands plan to open up about 20 000 000 hectares (over one and a half times the area of the United Kingdom) in Kazakhstan and Siberia. This vast expanse was divided into **sovkhozes** (State farms) owned and run by the Government. Unlike those on the kolkhozes, the sovkhoz workers did not earn their income by selling produce to the state but were paid wages as in a factory. Half a million young people were persuaded to settle in these vast regions in a movement which resembled the opening up of the West in the U.S.A. These pioneers lived in tents and rough shacks and often worked in very difficult conditions. The new corn lands were in areas of uncertain rainfall and they were farmed inefficiently. Although there were bumper crops in 1956 and 1958, harvests failed in other years. The 1963 harvest was so bad that it was necessary to ration bread and flour and to buy wheat abroad. Unfortunately this poor harvest led to the enforced slaughter of livestock, dramatically reversing the slow increase in the stock of farm animals.

Fig 18 Harvesting in the Virgin lands.

Khruschev also launched a scheme for increasing the output of maize. He developed great enthusiasm for maize, which could be used to fatten livestock as well as to feed people. This earned Khruschev the nickname of *Kukuruza,* the Russian word for maize. Although maize-growing was attempted in unsuitable regions, as in the Virgin Lands, in many areas it proved a useful crop. The production of fertilizers was increased by fifty per cent in five years in a further attempt to increase the yield of crops.

All this effort failed to achieve the hoped-for breakthrough in Russian agriculture. Khruschev's planning had been more imaginative than systematic and careful. Large areas of the Virgin Lands which were too dry to produce regular crops were quietly allowed to revert to pasture, and the emphasis moved back to increasing the fertility of the old corn lands.

The Seven Year Plan of 1959-1965 had anticipated an increase of 10 per cent a year in agricultural production. After six years the average increase was about 1 per cent, much less than in the earlier part of Khruschev's leadership.

Industry

In 1957 Khruschev announced a scheme for the reorganization of Russian industry. At the time all industrial enterprises were controlled by ministers in Moscow. Khruschev referred to 'the huge streams of paper coming from the ministries' which used up many workers and stifled the initiative of local factory managers. Now industry was to be run on a regional basis. The idea was that men on the spot who knew local problems would be able to organize more efficiently. The Government still decided what was to be produced; local people decided how this was to be done.

The new regions coincided with the areas of Communist Party organization; one of Khruschev's aims was to have industry under the eye of the Party. Khruschev's scheme has since been modified, but the basic idea of giving more power to the man on the spot has been retained.

The old system had at times depended on the activities of shadowy figures called 'fixers' who could arrange 'swops' between factories short of supplies, earning a side-profit for themselves. The Government usually turned a blind eye on the employment of fixers as long as a factory turned out its quota of goods.

Extra payments were given to factories producing more than their planned quota. Although this system often worked well, these payments were made whether the goods were wanted or not. At one time sewing machine factories were earning above-quota payments while retailers already had an enormous stock of $1\frac{1}{2}$ million machines. Also, payments did not depend on quality, which was often poor in the case of consumer goods. In 1964 a start was made in remedying this by relating some factory payments to quality as well as quantity.

In October 1957 the Russians launched the first unmanned **sputnik,** or space craft. A month later the dog Laika, in a space craft, orbited the world. Whatever the failures of Russian industry, here was dazzling proof of its scientific and technological advance. Space travel captured the imagination of the peoples of the world. Laika even began to appear on iced lollies and laundry vans in Great Britain. The U.S.S.R. had stolen a march on the U.S.A.: the space race was on. On 12 April 1961 Yuri Gagarin made the first manned space flight, orbiting the world at 28 800 k.p.h. He returned to a Red Square gay with banners where the outstretched arms of his leader awaited him. Khruschev delighted in sharing the glory of Soviet space triumphs.

Fig 19 Russian Spacecraft.

Fig 20 The engine room of the Volzhsky Lenin Hydro-electric Power Station.

When the Russian Government launched a new Seven Year Plan in 1959 they could already look back on impressive industrial growth after Stalin's death, a 50 per cent increase in production between 1954 and 1958. The 1959-1965 plan forecast a further 80 per cent increase in industrial output, and this was achieved. More details of industrial development in Khruschev's time are shown in the diagram. Although production in the U.S.S.R. seemed unlikely to fulfil Khruschev's hopes of overtaking that of the U.S.A. by 1970, it was certainly expanding more rapidly than that of its Western rival.

Economic Development In Khruschev's Time

	1954	1964
Steel	42 000 000 tonnes	85 000 000 tonnes
Crude oil	59 000 000 tonnes	224 000 000 tonnes
Cement	19 000 000 tonnes	65 000 000 tonnes
Cotton fabrics	5 590 000 000 metres	6 976 000 000 metres
Woollen cloth	159 000 tonnes	239 000 tonnes
Radios and televisions	3 154 000	4 766 000
Cars	95 000	185 000
Cattle	57 000 000	85 000 000
Sheep	99 000 000	134 000 000
Wheat	42 000 000 tonnes	74 000 000 tonnes

The development of heavy industry still held pride of place, but more stress was laid on producing consumer goods of fine quality. Khruschev believed that a Communist society should provide its members with a high standard of living.

Education

Stalin had separated boys and girls into different schools in 1943, but co-educational schools came into use again in 1954.

Khruschev once remarked that some pupils completed a course of secondary education without knowing one end of a hammer from the other. There followed in 1959 the 'Law Strengthening the Ties of School with Life'. School life was to be extended by a year (to the age of fifteen, although many Russians stayed beyond this) and more emphasis was to be placed on practical training. Boarding school education was to be greatly developed. It is interesting to note that these changes correspond to suggestions made in our own *Newsom Report* of 1963, which dealt with British secondary education. Not all Khruschev's educational reforms were entirely successful, however. Factory managers complained that young people sent from schools to gain experience of industrial work held back production.

In 1961 there were over 40 million Russians receiving full-time education, evening schools providing opportunities for many others. There were also $3\frac{1}{2}$ million children below the school age of seven attending kindergartens.

Of the $2\frac{1}{2}$ million students at universities and in other types of higher education, by far the greater number were studying sciences and engineering.

KHRUSCHEV'S RESIGNATION

Khruschev was never a dictator like Stalin who held all the strings of power in his own hands. In the last resort Khruschev had to rely on the support of the leadership of the Communist Party.

On the occasion of his seventieth birthday in 1964, Nikita Khruschev received the following greeting from the Communist Party and Government: 'Your devotion to the welfare of our motherland and of all progressive peoples has won you the profound respect and love of the Soviet people and of the workers of the world.'

15 October 1964 was a day of important news: a closely fought British general election and the exploding of China's first atomic bomb. To the Editor of the *London Evening News* came the hint of another major event, in a dispatch from his Moscow correspondent: 'Moscow is being decorated in preparation for welcoming the astronauts who come to the capital tomorrow. But missing from the usual portraits of government leaders is the well-known face of Mr. Khruschev.'

No confirmation of a change of leadership came from Moscow for some time. Finally the Russian Government announced that it had 'granted N. S. Khruschev's request that he be relieved of duties in view of advanced age and deterioration of health'. Before this bare announcement there had been no indication that Khruschev was planning to resign. In fact, he had probably been as surprised as anyone by the sudden turn of events.

Criticism of Khruschev had developed on a number of points: his handling of the Cuba crisis, undignified personal behaviour, the promotion of his son-in-law, inadequate development of heavy industry and the armed forces, his feud with Mao Tse-tung; no doubt his age and health were also taken into account. Khruschev's downfall was carefully planned. His opponents had sounded out the opinions of members of the Central Committee of the Communist Party before making their move, so that when Khruschev appealed to this body hoping for a repeat of his 1957 victory, he was voted down.

When the news broke in Moscow, there was no outbreak of the panic which had swept the city on Stalin's death. Khruschev had never aroused either the deep affection or the hatred which people had felt for the old leader.

For Khruschev there was to be no secret trial and sudden execution. Instead he was allowed to keep a flat in Moscow and a villa in the countryside, together with a few servants, until his death in 1971.

Khruschev was at the helm while the Russian people became somewhat freer and better off. He worked towards better relations with the West. One feels he deserves a significant place in Russian history.

The life of Khruschev

A SUMMARY

1894	Nikita Khruschev was born, son of a peasant, in the Ukraine.
1909	Worked in the Donbas coalmines.
1918	Joined the Bolsheviks.
1918–21	Fought in the Civil War.
1922	Death of his first wife in the famine.
1931	After study at college became a Communist Party official in Moscow.
1935–37	Organized the construction of the Moscow Metro.
1938	Became Chief of the Ukraine Communist Party.
1941–45	Led guerillas in the Ukraine.
1945–49	Put down anti-Communist groups in the Ukraine and took over the new lands from Poland.
1949	Took charge of Russia's agriculture — amalgamated collective farms.
1953	Became General Secretary of the Communist Party. Led the movement to reduce Government control over the people after Stalin's death.
1956	Made secret speech attacking Stalin.
1958	Became Prime Minister.
From 1953	Increased payments to collective farmers. Virgin Lands were opened up. Reduced the Central Government's control over industry. More consumer goods produced. Space programme developed. In foreign affairs followed policy of peaceful co-existence with the West despite the Cuba crisis (1962). Relations with China grew worse.
1964	Forced to resign due to general dissatisfaction with his leadership.

SUMMARY - Chapter 7

STALIN'S SUCCESSORS

Communist Party control of Russian life eased after Stalin's death. Malenkov became Prime Minister and General Secretary of the Party. Khruschev soon replaced him as General Secretary. Molotov, Zhukov and Beria were other prominent leaders. Beria, head of the hated secret police, was accused of spying and shot. Khruschev became Prime Minister also and thus emerged as Stalin's successor. He did not treat his rivals with Stalin's ruthlessness.

KHRUSCHEV'S EARLIER LIFE

Khruschev was born in South Russia in 1894. He worked on a farm as a child and had little education. At 15 he began work in the coalmines; the conditions there induced him to join the Communists. He fought for the Bolsheviks during the Civil War. In 1935 he became Secretary of the Moscow Communist Party. During the Second World War he was in charge of the Ukraine. Stalin made him Minister of Agriculture in 1949 and he reorganized the collective farms.

DE-STALINIZATION

At the 1956 Communist Party Congress, Khruschev criticized Stalin as a ruthless dictator who had led Russia badly during the war but he acknowledged Stalin's achievement in developing Russia's economy. Khruschev advocated the policy of peaceful co-existence with the West. People imprisoned by Stalin were released. Foreign visitors were allowed into the Soviet Union. Khruschev prevented authors producing books critical of the U.S.S.R. Following a further speech by Khruschev attacking Stalin in 1961, his statues were removed and Stalingrad renamed.

FOREIGN AFFAIRS – RELATIONS WITH THE WEST

During the 1950s, Russia developed the hydrogen bomb and long-range rockets. The great powers failed to agree on a scheme of disarmament. Khruschev made successful visits to Britain and the U.S.A. The U.S.A. discovered Russian missile sites in Cuba in 1962. War was avoided when Khruschev agreed to dismantle them. In the friendlier period which followed, the Moscow-New York 'hot line' was set up and the Test Ban Treaty made. Both the U.S.S.R. and U.S.A. gave aid to developing countries. They failed to agree on re-uniting East and West Germany, which became independent states in 1955. The East Germans built the Berlin Wall in 1961.

FOREIGN AFFAIRS – RELATIONS WITH OTHER COMMUNIST COUNTRIES
Although they crushed a rising in East Germany in 1953, the new Russian leaders relaxed control over the East European satellites. The Cominform was abolished in 1956. A liberal Communist, Gomulka, became the Polish leader. Russian troops prevented the establishment of a non-Communist government in Hungary. China rejected Khruschev's policy of peaceful co-existence with the West and challenged the U.S.S.R.'s leadership of World Communism.

UNITED NATIONS
Russia joined more of the specialized agencies of the U.N. but refused to participate in its peace-keeping activities.

AGRICULTURE
Khruschev greatly increased government payments to collective farms. The 'Virgin Lands' scheme to open up huge areas of central U.S.S.R. for corn growing was only partly successful. The hoped-for breakthrough in agricultural production did not occur.

INDUSTRY
Khruschev's reforms of 1957 gave more control over industry to local managers. An unmanned Soviet space craft was launched in 1957. In 1961, Gagarin made the first manned space flight. Industrial production increased $2\frac{1}{2}$ times between 1954 and 1964. More consumer goods were manufactured and attempts were made to improve their quality.

EDUCATION
Co-educational schools were re-introduced and more emphasis was placed on practical training. The minimum leaving age was raised to 15. Higher education was extended, particularly in engineering and the sciences.

KHRUSCHEV'S RESIGNATION
Khruschev's position was never as strong as Stalin's, and in 1964 he was forced to resign. His age and ill-health were the official reasons but his policies on industry, Cuba and China were other factors. Khruschev was allowed to live in peaceful retirement until his death in 1971. Russians had become freer and better off during his period of leadership.

Russia after Khruschev

8

THE NEW LEADERS

In 1964 no one person took Khruschev's place. Three men emerged in the front rank of leadership: Alexander Kosygin, Leonid Brezhnev and Nikolai Podgorny.

Kosygin, born in 1904, was Khruschev's successor as Prime Minister. He differed from Stalin and Khruschev in owing his earlier promotion to successful experience in industry. He was the manager of a spinning mill before becoming an official of the Communist Party in 1938. Even then, he concentrated on economic problems, becoming one of Stalin's inner group of advisers. Later he was a key figure in Khruschev's government. His criticism of his leader's economic policies was probably an important factor in Khruschev's downfall. When Kosygin

Fig 21 Nikita Khruschev (right) with Leonard Brezhnev.

visited Britain in 1967, he created a favourable impression by his personality and intelligence when interviewed on television and by his kindly behaviour towards ordinary people.

Brezhnev, who took over from Khruschev as General Secretary of the Communist Party, was less well known in the West. Born in 1906, he was once an engineer, becoming a full time official of the Communist Party in 1950. By 1957 he had reached the top group of leaders under Khruschev. In 1960, Brezhnev became President of the U.S.S.R. but he exchanged this post for the more influential one of Communist Party leader in 1964. There were for a time reports of disagreement between Brezhnev, who was believed to wish to restore something of Stalin's reputation, and the more moderate Kosygin. Brezhnev's visit to the U.S.A. and the way that his image has been built up by the Soviet press have confirmed the impression that at the present time (June 1974), he is the most influential of Russia's leaders. But he has his critics and the situation could change at any time.

Nikolai Podgorny, President of the U.S.S.R., was born in 1903. He trained as an engineer and, like Khruschev, was once General Secretary of the Ukraine Communist Party. He was one of Khruschev's chief lieutenants before the latter's resignation. In 1965 he became President and, not content with being a mere figurehead, has taken an active part in government policy making, although apparently lacking the influence of Brezhnev and Kosygin.

The Government and the people

On Khruschev's downfall, some people who owed their position to his personal influence were dismissed. These included his son-in-law, editor of the newspaper *Izvestia*. There was no widespread purge.

Fig 22 Alexander
Solzhenitsyn,
Nobel Prize
winning novelist.

The new leaders reacted strongly to criticism of Communist Party policy. Two authors, Siniavsky and Daniel, who had published abroad under the pseudonyms of Terts and Arzhak, were accused of anti-Soviet activities, and were arrested and imprisoned. Their works were all fictional comments on modern Soviet society and while they might be considered quite critical they were not necessarily anti-Soviet, and did not attack the Soviet government. Their fate led to widespread protests both inside and outside Russia and they were eventually released. Alexander Solzhenitsyn, the author of *First Circle, Cancer Ward, One Day in the Life of Ivan Denisovich, August 1914* and *Gulag Archipelago,* the most famous of living Russian writers, has suffered considerably for his critical descriptions of life in the Soviet Union. He is not allowed to have his novels published in the U.S.S.R. although they are circulated illegally among his sympathisers via **samizdat**. Solzhenitsyn achieved widespread acclaim in the West and in 1970 was awarded the Nobel Prize for Literature. However, owing to government disapproval and the possibility of re-entry into the Soviet Union proving difficult, he declined to attend the presentation ceremony in Stockholm. In 1974, Solzhenitsyn was expelled from the U.S.S.R. after the publication of an 'open' letter in which he condemned the policies of the Communist Government. His name is now a symbol of opposition to the Soviet Government.

The Soviet Constitution states 'Freedom of religious worship and freedom of anti-religious propaganda is recognised for all citizens.' Nevertheless there have been recent reports of Baptists being sentenced to long terms of imprisonment for running Sunday schools. The Russian Orthodox Church which had a measure of freedom restored during the war years and tends to co-operate with the Government is allowed to function. Of the 400 churches in Moscow in 1917, only two dozen are open for services. Some Russians are still Christians but many have deserted that faith for another; the peasant's icon illuminated by candles has often been replaced by a picture of Lenin lit by an electric bulb. Mrs. Wilson, the British Prime Minister's wife, visiting Lenin's mausoleum in 1966, observed 'the expression of awe and adoration on their faces as they file past the tomb having waited for hours in the endless queue which winds across Red Square . . . this is the faith which becomes their religion.'

Fig 23 Red Square, Moscow.

Minority races have continued to demand a greater degree of freedom and have suffered for their efforts. Some of the Jewish population have been sacked from their jobs after asking permission to emigrate to Israel. Because of well-organized support from abroad, the Jews have had some success. But the Government resents that anyone should wish to give up the privilege of being a Soviet citizen. In 1970, two Lithuanians hijacked a Soviet airliner and forced the pilot to fly to Turkey. There were riots in Lithuania in 1972. The Crimean Tartars, expelled from the Crimea to Central Asia after the war, have never given up the struggle to return to their homeland. Hundreds have been arrested and General Grigorenko who has led the Tartar protests has been declared insane and sent to a mental hospital. The Government policy of treating political opponents as psychiatric cases has been bitterly criticized.

Although the Russians may complain of injustices by local officials and farm or factory managers, they must accept rule by the Communist Party. In the elections to the Supreme Soviet (the Russian Parliament) in 1966 as usual only candidates approved by the Communist Party were allowed. The Supreme Soviet only meets a few days each year and has little real power. The task of members of the Government is to carry out the instructions of the Communist Party. As Lenin once said: 'The Party is the brain and the Government is the body'.

The Communist Party consists of about 5 to 6 per cent of the whole population, although all important decisions are made by the small numbers of leaders who make up the Politburo, its ruling committee. Communist Party membership is restricted to those who are prepared to work actively for the Party as organisers and to build up support for its policies. Some hope to gain promotion in their jobs by appearing to be keen Communists, others act out of sincere personal belief. To be appointed to important posts in the civil service and armed forces as to do certain other jobs, including history teaching, it is essential to be a member of the Communist Party. About 23 million young people aged between 14 and 26 belong to the **Komsomol,** the youth movement associated with the Communist Party.

Agriculture

The key problem of agriculture received special attention from the new leaders. The collective farms have been reorganized into larger units and the total area cultivated by them has been reduced. The total area cultivated by the state farms has increased sixfold since 1953 so that it is now greater than that of the collective farms. It is presumably believed that agriculture can be made more efficient if farm management comes more directly under government control. While farms have become larger to permit more effective control of production and use of machinery, experiments have been conducted in splitting up the labour force into small teams of as few as six men who could work more as family groups.

There is a vivid contrast between Stalin's methods of compulsion

106

and terror and the recent use of money incentives. The 1966 Five Year Plan anticipated a 25 per cent increase in agricultural production. It also proposed a 40 per cent increase in wages for collective farmers, twice the amount for town workers. In fact, one pay award given in July 1966 was more than the amount planned for the whole five year period: the income of some of the poorer kolkhozes was increased by as much as 60 per cent. In addition, restrictions on the use of private plots have been removed. This is the most thorough-going attempt so far to win the support of the peasants. The encouragement is certainly needed as farmworkers still earn less than factory workers. The drift to the towns of the younger workers has resulted in the average age of farmworkers rising to almost fifty.

Despite all efforts, agriculture has remained the weak link in the Soviet economy. Not all the blame can be laid at the feet of the Russian planners and farmers although machinery is still in short supply and poorly maintained. There have been some disastrous cold winters and dry summers; in 1972 the Minister of Agriculture said that conditions were the worst of the century. Serious grain shortages have been avoided by imports from North America but in the autumn of 1972 there were long queues for bread and meat in some towns.

Industry and living standards

In industry, as in agriculture, the over-ambitious targets set by Khruschev were quietly laid aside by the new leaders. Not that Khruschev was alone in his optimism: Prime Minister Wilson's 'National Plan' and President Johnson's 'Great Society' suffered similar fates.

The plan for 1966-1970 was nevertheless ambitious enough, proposing a far faster rate of economic growth than that of Russia's Western rivals. The aim to raise industrial output 50 per cent by 1970 was achieved according to official sources, although some doubts were expressed on this claim by Western experts. Kosygin has predicted that the long awaited moment when Russia's output in industry and agriculture will exceed that of the United States will occur in 1975. Previous predictions by Soviet leaders on this subject have proved over-optimistic, so this one must be treated with caution.

In 1972 Russia began to show as much interest as the West in environmental problems. It launched schemes to prevent air pollution and to preserve natural resources.

Discipline in industry has been tightened. A campaign has been launched against workers who are lazy, take too many days off and particularly those who drink too much. Alcoholism has recently received the same sort of criticism in Russian newspapers as drug taking has been given in the Western press. There is a good deal of evidence, however, that failings in industry are at least as much the result of incompetent managers as poor workers. Dissatisfaction with working arrangements has led to very large numbers of people changing their jobs.

The Soviet leaders laid special stress on the need to improve living

Fig 24 A young
woman
construction
worker (women
tackle many jobs
which are done
only by men in
western
countries).

standards by producing good quality consumer goods. No longer would
it be good enough to mass-produce shoddy articles which were left to
gather dust on the shelves. The latest Five Year Plan, announced in
1971, stated that consumer goods were to increase by 50 per cent.

The *Observer's* Moscow correspondent commented in March 1967 on
the improving standard of living: 'This winter it has usually been
possible to get oranges, apples and even bananas in quite ordinary
shops outside the city centre. This was not so two years ago. The young
people are noticeably better dressed.' Some shortages still persisted: 'It
is not that people don't have the money; the supply of luxury goods is

behind demand and even a box of three minute bottles of Chanel perfume costing £24 that I saw in Gorky Street will probably find a buyer.' The hoped-for increase in the supply of consumer goods has not been fully attained and later visitors have confirmed the impression given above.

The Government has planned a vast building programme for the next few years. Many people still live in cramped conditions sharing bathrooms and kitchens with other families. Nevertheless many families in Moscow and other large towns have been allocated small, modern, self-contained flats. Brezhnev declared in 1973 'We want to make our towns and villages more comfortable to live in and more beautiful.'

The Russian worker as he becomes more prosperous is beginning to think of owning a car. At the moment this is quite unusual. In 1964 it was estimated that only one person in 300 owned a car in Russia, compared with one in eight in Britain and one in three in the U.S.A. In order to boost car production, the Government arranged for the Italian Fiat Company to build a giant automobile factory in the U.S.S.R., at a place known as Togliatti (named after a well-known Italian Socialist).

FOREIGN AFFAIRS — RELATIONS WITH NON-COMMUNIST COUNTRIES

Kosygin appeared in the role of skilful peacemaker in January 1966 when he persuaded the leaders of India and Pakistan, who were fighting over Kashmir, to negotiate a truce. When war broke out again between India and Pakistan in 1971, China accused Russia of encouraging India to begin the fighting. Nevertheless, the Soviet leaders have endeavoured to keep on good terms with and extend their influence in both India and Pakistan.

In the Desert War of the summer of 1967, the Russians supported the Arabs in their unsuccessful attempt to crush Israel. As in Vietnam, this support came in the forms of propaganda, equipment and technical advice rather than actual involvement in the fighting. Since then the Egyptians have shown a suspicion of Communist influence, expelling all Russian military experts in 1973.

Khruschev's policy of peaceful co-existence with the West has been followed by his successors — at first cautiously and then with increasing confidence and sense of purpose. In 1967 an agreement was made between the U.S.A., Britain and U.S.S.R. not to put outer space to military use. A treaty of 1971 between the three powers banned nuclear weapons from the sea-bed.

In 1972 and 1973 there was an exchange of visits between the American and Russian leaders. In May 1972, after talks in the Kremlin, Nixon and Brezhnev agreed to bring to an end the nuclear arms race after 25 years of fantastically expensive competition. The agreement did not include an effective system of inspection, so it could in fact be dishonoured by either side. Although the U.S.S.R. continued firmly to condemn American intervention in Vietnam, there was clearly an improvement in the relationship between the two super-powers.

In the summer of 1973 a smiling Mr. Brezhnev stood at President Nixon's side in the Western White House in California. They had signed an agreement on the prevention of nuclear war which Brezhnev described as 'a document of historic importance'. Other agreements planned co-operation covering an impressive range of activities. These included agriculture, transportation, world ocean studies and cultural exchanges. To assist in the long term expansion of trade between the two countries, ten large American companies were to set up offices in the Soviet Union.

The coming together of Brezhnev and Nixon was not just a sudden outburst of brotherly love, but forced upon them by serious economic problems which co-operation could help to solve. The U.S.S.R. has a surplus of raw materials and natural gas which the U.S.A. needs, and which can be more rapidly exploited with finance and technical skills from the U.S.A. American industry would like a new market for manufactured goods. Both had to face up to the fact that the emergence of other major powers: the European Community, China and Japan, lessened the influence of the U.S.S.R. and U.S.A. They came together in a sense for mutual protection. The peace agreement in Vietnam early in 1973 which led to the withdrawal of American troops helped to improve relations between Russia and America. Both countries emphasized the need for the ceasefire in Vietnam to be observed.

One cannot be sure that the new spirit of friendship will last. However, Brezhnev in his parting speech before leaving the U.S.A. showed no doubt: 'Mankind has outgrown the rigid armour of the Cold War . . . It wants to breathe freely and peacefully . . . Dear Americans, please accept my good wishes for prosperity and happiness for all of you'. Such kindly sentiments are not extended to critics of Communism in Russia.

Britain's relations with the U.S.S.R. have not so far improved in line with the U.S.A.'s. In September 1971, over a hundred Russian officials living in Britain were accused of spying and expelled from the country. By 1973, the relationship between the two countries appeared friendlier with the visit of Prince Philip to Moscow.

The U.S.S.R.'s policy of widening its links throughout the world resulted in 1972 in trade treaties with West Germany and Japan. Japan is at the moment the Soviet Union's chief trading partner in the capitalist world.

Agreements first made between the U.S.S.R., West Germany and East Germany in 1970 came into full effect in 1972. Under these, the three countries agreed to respect their existing frontiers. This implied that Germany was giving up all claims to a third of its pre-war territories. The friendlier relations between East and West Germany led to a relaxation of travel restrictions and to more trade between them.

110

The new leaders tried at first to re-establish Communist unity by ending the feud with China, but despite their efforts, the old national rivalry has continued. In March 1969, some scores of men were killed during fighting in the border region of the Ussuri River. Feelings ran high on both sides, whipped up by official propaganda. The Chinese radio reported waves of demonstrators marching to the Russian embassy in Peking 'with the fire of anger in their hearts' shouting 'Down with the new Tsars!' The quarrel was temporarily patched up after a meeting of the Russian and Chinese Prime Ministers. However, in 1972 the Russians complained that the New Chinese Atlas showed $1\frac{1}{2}$ million square kilometres of U.S.S.R. territory as belonging to China.

Until the summer of 1968, it seemed that Russia's new Government had reluctantly decided to allow the East European Communist states to develop along their own lines. In Czechoslovakia, the popular government led by Dubcek freed the Press from state control and planned economic reform. To the Russian Government, it seemed that Czechoslovakia was set on a path which would lead it away from Communism and would weaken the Warsaw Defence Pact. On the night of August 21, without warning, Soviet troops poured into Czechoslovakia. Some patriots took to arms but the Czechoslovak government, anxious to avoid a blood-bath, pleaded with their people not to resist. The Czechoslovaks were forced to abandon reforms and freedom of the Press. In 1969, the Russian-backed Husak replaced Dubcek as Prime Minister. The Russian troops, unwelcome guests who claim to have been invited in to 'protect' Czechoslovakia are still there at the time of writing (1975). The Czechoslovaks have maintained their contempt for the invaders, treating as a shrine the place where Jan Palach, a 21 year old student, burned himself to death as a protest at the Russian occupation and the stamping out of freedom.

The invasion of Czechoslovakia brought dismay to East Europeans, particularly the Rumanians, who were gradually freeing themselves from Russian control. Shortly after the invasion, Brezhnev justified it by stating what has been called the 'Brezhnev Doctrine': that Socialist states, having reached, according to Marxist teaching, a higher state of development, could not be allowed to go back to pre-Socialist conditions. Mao Tse-tung commented that the Russians were 'enforcing Fascist dictatorship at home and carrying out aggression and expansion abroad'.

The Czechoslovak invasion set back for a time the closer relationship developing between the Soviet Union and the West. But, as in the case of Hungary, the Western powers only protested. They accepted in fact that the Russians had special rights over East European Communist states as Brezhnev claimed. This attitude encouraged the Russian leaders in extending their links with the West once feelings over Czechoslovakia had died down.

———— U. S. S. R. Frontier

—·—·— S. S. R. (Soviet Socialist
Republic) frontier

0   500   1000   1500   2000 km

0   500   1000 miles

Map 8 The Soviet
Union today

The pre-revolutionary Russian Empire and the USSR today

The true Communist society which Karl Marx described was based on the principle of: 'From each according to his ability, to each according to his need.' All class divisions and national divisions were to have disappeared. There was to be no need for a government as society would have reached a perfect balance and would run itself like a superbly regulated machine.

The U.S.S.R. today has not reached this goal. Nor could it apparently do so unless Communism became world-wide. In fact, the ideal Communist society appears a distant dream far removed from the present problems and policies of the Soviet Union.

Nevertheless, Russia has been transformed in many ways during the last half century. In particular, she has changed from an agricultural to an industrial nation; from a land of peasants to one of mainly town workers. The tables on page 113 show some of the principal changes.

It can be said quite definitely that the average Russian is today much better paid, better fed, better educated, twice as long-lived and provided with far finer social services than in Tsar Nicholas II's time. But he still has not the power to choose the government which rules him. He lacks the freedom to write and say what he believes.

The ordinary Russian has not reached the standard of living of the advanced countries of the West but he has caught up with them to a considerable extent. On the other hand, he has outstripped the backward countries of Europe like Portugal and has left far behind the underdeveloped lands of Asia and Africa.

Before the Revolution and Today

A comparison based on the figures of 1913 and 1970

	1913	1970
POPULATION	159 million	242 million
INDUSTRIAL PRODUCTION		
Coal	29 million tonnes	433 million tonnes
Oil	10 million tonnes	353 million tonnes
Crude Steel	4 million tonnes	116 million tonnes
Electricity	2 billion kilowatt hours	740 billion kilowatt hours
Cotton textiles	1817 million metres	6653 million metres
Clocks and watches	1 million	40 million
AGRICULTURAL PRODUCTION		
Grain	86 million tonnes	162 million tonnes
Potatoes	32 million tonnes	97 million tonnes
Cattle	58 million	95 million
HEALTH		
Death rate	30 per thousand	8 per thousand
Infant death rate	273 per thousand	24 per thousand
Hospital beds	207 thousand	2567 thousand
Doctors	28 thousand	555 thousand
EDUCATION		
Teachers	280 thousand	$2\frac{1}{2}$ million
Pupils	10 million	49 million

U.S.S.R., U.S.A., CHINA AND U.K.

An economic comparison based on 1970 production figures

	U.S.S.R.	U.S.A.	CHINA	U.K.
POPULATION	242 million	205 million	760 million	55 million
Crude oil	353 million tonnes	475 million tonnes	24 million tonnes	0.1 million tonnes
Crude steel	116 million tonnes	119 million tonnes	17 million tonnes	28 million tonnes
Electricity output	740 billion kilowatt hours	1638 billion kilowatt hours	14 billion kilowatt hours	249 billion kilowatt hours
Radio receivers	7815 thousand	14 271 thousand	3754 thousand	1303 thousand
Cars	344 thousand	6547 thousand	8 thousand	1641 thousand
Cattle	95 million	112 million	63 million	13 million
Pigs	56 million	57 milllion	223 million	8 million
Grain	162 million tonnes	168 million tonnes	129 million tonnes	13 million tonnes
Tractors/combined harvesters in use	2000 thousand	4770 thousand	165 thousand	352 thousand

SUMMARY – Chapter 8

THE NEW LEADERS

After Khruschev's fall, Alexei Kosygin, Leonid Brezhnev and Nikolai Podgorny were the most prominent leaders. All had careers in industry before becoming Communist Party officials. Kosygin became Prime Minister, Brezhnev General Secretary of the Communist Party, and Podgorny President of the U.S.S.R. Brezhnev appears at present to be the most important of the Soviet leaders.

THE GOVERNMENT AND THE PEOPLE

Some people who owed their jobs to Khruschev's influence were sacked by the government. There has been increasingly strict government control of the population. Religious freedom is limited. Some critics of the government and minority races have been persecuted. The only political party allowed is the Communist Party. It controls Parliament and fills key jobs.

AGRICULTURE

Collective farms have been increased in size but reduced in number and there has been a great increase in the area cultivated by state farms. To win the support of the farm workers and to stem the drift to the towns, there have been large wage increases. Partly because of climatic conditions, agricultural production has been low and food has been imported.

INDUSTRY AND LIVING STANDARDS

The government aimed to raise output by 50 per cent in the plan for 1966-70. It has been claimed that this target was reached overall. Environmental problems have received some attention. Discipline at work has been tightened. Living standards and the housing situation have somewhat improved. Although efforts have been made to greatly increase the production of consumer goods, there are still shortages.

FOREIGN AFFAIRS – RELATIONS WITH NON-COMMUNIST COUNTRIES

Russia has endeavoured to extend her influence in India and Pakistan. She supported the Arabs in their conflict with Israel. The policy of peaceful co-existence with the West has been extended. This reached a peak with the agreement on the prevention of nuclear war signed during Brezhnev's visit to the U.S.A. in 1973. The rise of China and Japan, economic problems and the cease-fire in Vietnam helped to bring Russia and America together. Britain's relationship with Russia has not run so smoothly. West Germany, East Germany and Russia have agreed to respect their existing frontiers. The U.S.S.R. has extended her trade with the Capitalist world.

FOREIGN AFFAIRS – RELATIONS WITH COMMUNIST COUNTRIES
Attempts to end the rivalry with China have failed and there was border fighting in 1969. Under what has since been called the 'Brezhnev Doctrine', Soviet troops occupied Czechoslovakia in 1968. They installed a pro-Russian government and stayed there. The Western powers and China protested but took no other action. The invasion checked changes in other East European states.

TSARIST RUSSIA AND RUSSIA TODAY
The U.S.S.R. has not attained the Communist society envisaged by Marx. Nevertheless, there have been great changes. Russia has changed from an agricultural to an industrial nation. The average Russian's standard of living and education are far better than in Tsarist times but he is still not able to freely elect his own leaders or express his own opinions.

Questions

In answering the following questions, refer to books other than *Russia in the Twentieth Century* wherever possible. (See the bibliography on page 127.)

Chapter 1
(1) On an outline map of the U.S.S.R., mark in:
    (a) the natural zones
    (b) the principal rivers and mountain ranges.
(2) Write a few sentences about each of the following:
    (a) the size of the U.S.S.R.
    (b) the climate
    (c) the number and variety of the peoples.
(3) Describe the life of Russian peasants in 1900.
(4) Write about Russia's industries and workers in 1900, covering the following points:
    (a) a comparison of Russia's industrial development with that of the West
    (b) the part played by the Government
    (c) railway development
    (d) working conditions
    (e) trade unions.
(5) Write a character study of Tsar Nicholas II.
(6) Explain Russia's system of government in 1900.

Chapter 2
(1) Write a short biography of Karl Marx, explaining his main political ideas.
(2) Describe Lenin's life up to the year 1903.
(3) What happened at the following places during the Russo-Japanese War:
    (a) Port Arthur
    (b) Tsushima
    (c) Mukden?
(4) Imagine that you were a worker marching in Father Gapon's procession. Describe your thoughts and tell the story of the events which followed.
(5) Write a few sentences about each of the following:
    (a) why the Duma was first called by the Tsar
    (b) the voting system for the Duma
    (c) the powers of the Duma
    (d) Stolypin's agricultural reforms.

(6) (a) Explain Rasputin's influence over the Royal Family.
    (b) What part did Rasputin play in the government of Russia?
    (c) Why and how was he assassinated?
(7) What reasons can you find for the overthrow of the Tsar in 1917?
(8) Suppose that you were living in Petrograd during the summer and autumn of 1917. Describe the events which took place.

Chapter 3

(1) Write a paragraph about each of the following:
    (a) the Decree on Peace and Land
    (b) the Constituent Assembly
    (c) the Treaty of Brest-Litovsk.
(2) Write an account of the Civil War including the following points:
    (a) Allied support for the White Armies
    (b) the campaigns of Kornilov, Denikin and Admiral Kolchak
    (c) the murder of the Royal Family
    (d) the reasons for the Bolsheviks's victory.
(3) (a) Describe the difficulties which Lenin faced in organizing agriculture and industry.
    (b) Explain the significance of the New Economic Policy.
(4) On an outline map, mark Russia's frontiers in 1914. Shade in and name the areas which were no longer Russian in 1921.
(5) Write a few sentences about each of the following:
    (a) the Comintern
    (b) the Russo-Polish War
    (c) the Treaty of Rapallo.

Chapter 4

(1) Describe Stalin's life until 1924.
(2) Give an account of Stalin's policy of industrialization up to 1940. Mention the aims, difficulties and achievements. Use production figures to back up some of your statements.
(3) (a) Why did Stalin wish to 'collectivize' Russia's farms?
    (b) Why did the peasants resist so strongly?
    (c) How successful were Stalin's agricultural policies?
(4) In which ways did Stalin continue and in which ways did he change the social policies begun under Lenin?
(5) Write an account of the purges of the 1930s:
    (a) as a supporter of Stalin might have described them
    (b) as a supporter of Trotsky might have described them.

Chapter 5

(1) List in two columns in date order the successes and the failures of Stalin's foreign policies between 1924 and 1933.
(2) What were the reasons for:
    (a) the Popular Front
    (b) the Anti-Comintern Pact
    (c) the Russo-German Treaty
    (d) the Russian invasion of Finland?

(3) Write a paragraph about each of the following aspects of the war:
    (a) the German advances of 1941
    (b) Stalin's efforts to secure national unity
    (c) German atrocities
    (d) the siege of Leningrad.
(4) Describe Russia's part in the war from the Battle of Stalingrad until Germany's surrender.

Chapter 6

(1) On an outline map of Europe, mark in:
    (a) the lands which the U.S.S.R. gained as a result of the war
    (b) the satellite states in which Communist governments were established.
(2) Write a few sentences about each of the following:
    (a) Stalin and Tito
    (b) the Berlin air lift
    (c) the Communist take-over in China
    (d) the Vietnam War
    (e) the Korean War.
(3) Give an account of the steps which were taken to develop the Soviet Union's farms and industries after the war.
(4) Describe the way in which Stalin ruled the U.S.S.R. in his last years, explaining the reasons for his actions.

Chapter 7

(1) Make a time-chart showing the changes in leadership between 1953 and 1958 mentioned in the section 'Stalin's Successors'.
(2) Write an account of Khruschev's life up to 1953.
(3) Describe the process of de-Stalinization mentioning:
    (a) the things for which Khruschev blamed Stalin in his 1956 speech
    (b) the achievements of Stalin which he acknowledged
    (c) the excuse that Khruschev gave for the leaders who had obeyed Stalin
    (d) the changes in everyday life that followed Khruschev's speech
    (e) the attempts made to limit criticism of the Government.
(4) Make a list in date order of the events in the section 'Foreign affairs – relations with the West'.
(5) Explain the changes which took place in the U.S.S.R.'s relations with the East European satellite states and with China while Khruschev was in power.
(6) Describe Khruschev's agricultural policies and estimate their success.
(7) Write paragraphs on each of the following:
    (a) changes in the management of industry
    (b) changes in payments to industry
    (c) space flights
    (d) industrial growth during Khruschev's leadership.

Chapter 8

(1) Describe briefly the careers of Kosygin, Brezhnev and Podgorny.
(2) Write an account of the agricultural and industrial policies followed by the new leadership.
(3) Describe the policies of Russia's new leaders towards other Communist states, mentioning particularly China and Czechoslovakia.
(4) What events have indicated a 'thaw' in the Cold War between Russia and the U.S.A.? Why has this thaw occurred?

GENERAL REVISION QUESTIONS

(1) Using the summary of his life as a framework, write a biography of Lenin.
(2) Compare the life of a Russian factory worker or peasant in 1900 with that of one today.
(3) Would you have preferred to live in Russia under Tsar Nicholas II or under Stalin? Give reasons for your answer.
(4) Explain why Russians generally supported the Tsar in declaring war in 1914, but were disillusioned with the war and with him in 1917.
(5) Using the summary of his life as a framework, write a biography of Stalin.
(6) Write a brief account of the careers of two of the following:
    (a) Stolypin
    (b) Rasputin
    (c) Kerensky
    (d) Trotsky.
(7) (a) Describe the way in which the U.S.S.R. is governed today.
    (b) Describe the way in which Russia was ruled in 1900.
    (c) Why do you think Russia has never had a democratic government of the Western type?
(8) Both Lenin and Stalin took ruthless steps as head of Russia's Government. Describe these and consider which of them could be justified.
(9) Explain:
    (a) why the Russians started the war badly in 1941
    (b) why they finally defeated the Germans.
(10) Compare Russia's position after the First World War in 1918 with her position after the Second World War in 1945. Explain why she was so much stronger on the latter occasion.
(11) Should Russia or the West bear the blame for the outbreak of the Cold War?
(12) Mark on an outline map of South East Asia, countries which have become Communist since the Second World War. Write a short account of the history of two of these countries since 1945.
(13) Using the summary of his life as a framework, write a biography of Khruschev.

(14) Describe the development of Russian agriculture since 1917, explaining why progress has been slow.

(15) Write an account of the growth of Russia's industries under the Communists, explaining the emphasis on heavy industry and the slow rise in living standards.

(16) Describe the development of the U.S.S.R.'s health and educational services.

Glossary

ANTI-PARTY GROUP. The expression use to describe the leaders who opposed Khruschev's rise to power.

BOLSHEVIK. Russian for 'member of the majority'. The expression was used to describe the majority group of the Social Democratic Party led by Lenin after the split in 1903. The Bolsheviks later became the Communist Party.

CAPITALISM. The system in which the industries of a country are owned by a small group of people (the capitalists) who hire the labour of the class who own little or no property (the working class).

CHEKA. The secret police force set up by the Bolsheviks under Lenin. It was a descendant of the dreaded *Ochrana*, the Tsarist police force begun by Nicholas I. Some members were criminals released at the time of the revolution. Many took part in the murders and looting then frequent in Petrograd. The Cheka later gave rise to the notorious OGPU, the political police force.

COLLECTIVE FARM or KOLKHOZ. A large farm owned and worked collectively by all its members and which in the U.S.S.R. has to sell a certain amount of its produce to the Government at fixed prices.

COMINFORM. Communist Information Bureau. The organization set up after the Second World War to co-ordinate the activities of the European Communist Parties. It was disbanded in 1956 to help better relations with the West.

COMINTERN. Communist International. The body set up in 1919 by Russia to organize foreign Communist revolutions. The Comintern was ended in 1943 as a gesture to Russia's war-time allies.

COMMUNES. An early attempt by the Tsarist government to give limited freedom to the peasant community. Under a law passed by Tsar Alexander II, village groups were allocated plots of land for which they were expected to make repayments. These communes, largely due to poor farming methods, were mostly unsuccessful.

COMMUNISM. A system of government intended to create the ideal society towards which the Russians claim to be moving. In this ideal Communist society there would be no class divisions; people would work at the jobs to which they were best suited, receiving in return all that they needed, without payment. The word 'Communism' is more loosely used to describe the form of society actually in existence in Russia today.

COMMUNIST PARTY. At present the ruling (and only) political body in the U.S.S.R. Party membership consists of 5 to 6 per cent of the total population. All important decisions are made by a select group of leaders (see Politburo).

CONSUMER GOODS. Goods such as clothes and furniture bought for personal use by ordinary people.

DE-STALINIZATION. The process of removing the strict Government control which Stalin enforced over many aspects of everyday life.

DUMA. The form of elected Parliament introduced by the Tsar after the 1905 Revolution which lasted until 1917. The upper classes were over-represented and the Duma's actions were subject to the Tsar's approval.

GUERILLAS or *PARTISANS.* People who continue the fight against the enemy who has occupied their country by acts of sabotage, murder and small-scale military operations.

HAEMOPHILIA. An hereditary disease from which the son of Tsar Alexander II suffered. The gravest effects of the disease are excessive bleeding even from the most minor injury.

ICON. A picture of a saint or other holy person itself regarded as sacred and worshipped.

IRON CURTAIN. Churchill's expression used to describe the barriers set up by Communist Countries after the Second World War to separate their peoples from those of Western Europe.

KOLKHOZ. See *COLLECTIVE FARM.*

KOMSOMOL. The Communist Youth Organisation with over 23 million members aged between 14 and 26. Its primary aim is to promote communist ideology; it also runs clubs, summer camps and art centres and promotes sporting activities.

KREMLIN. The buildings in Moscow which house the Government Offices.

KULAK. These were the wealthy land-owning peasants who worked large farms using some machinery and employed labour. They provided the surplus agricultural produce which the poorer peasants could not. Their actions in 1927/8 showed they were unwilling to part with this surplus on the terms the State was willing to offer.

MAUSOLEUM. A stately tomb.

MENSHEVIK. Russian for 'member of the minority'. Used to describe the smaller group of the Social Democratic Party after the split in 1903. They were more moderate than the Bolsheviks and prepared to work with other parties for the overthrow of the Tsar.

MINORITY RACES. National groups, such as Georgians and Tartars, who are much less numerous than the Slavs, who make up most of Russia's population.

MOUJIK. A Russian peasant. Under Tsarist rule the peasant classes were victims of serfdom. Property of the estate owners, they could be bought and sold and only retained a right to farm small plots of land given in exchange for their labour.

NAZI. Abbreviation for National Socialist, the party led by Hitler which claimed the Germans were a master race. It was anti-Communist and anti-Jewish.

PARTISAN. See *GUERILLA.*

PEACEFUL CO-EXISTENCE. The way in which Communist and non-Communist countries live together without war but not really in friendship.

PETITION. A written request that some grievance be put right.

POGROM. An organized attack on a particular section of the population especially the Jews.

POLITBURO. An assembly of top Communist Party members, the real executive authority being held by its chairman.

POPULAR FRONT. The co-operation of Communists with other political parties against the Nazis and their supporters.

PRAVDA. The official Communist Party daily newspaper having a circulation of around 6 000 000. Like *Izvestia*, the government daily paper, and other leading organs, it adheres closely to the lines laid down by the State and Party.

PROPAGANDA. Information presented to the public through newspapers, broadcasts, books and films, and which favours a particular point of view. A very one-sided viewpoint is presented and the truth is often lost sight of or deliberately ignored.

PROVISIONAL GOVERNMENT. The government set up in 1917 by the Duma after the Tsar's abdication.

RED ARMY. The army of Communist Russia, now called the Soviet Army in the U.S.S.R. Originally the *Bolshevik Army*, successfully led by Trotsky during the Civil War. It was made up of volunteers who elected their own officers. Later, officers of the old Tsarist army were pressed into service.

SAMIZDAT. This practice of 'self-publishing', although not strictly illegal, is naturally discouraged, especially since the content is material which the censors would not normally pass for publication.

SATELLITE STATES. The countries of eastern Europe which were under Russian control after the Second World War.

SECOND FRONT. The attack launched against the Germans in 1944 in Western Europe which had been long demanded by the Russians.

SOCIAL DEMOCRATIC PARTY. The revolutionary Russian political party set up in 1898 which split into the Bolshevik and Menshevik groups.

SOCIALIST. Someone who believes that the Government should control a country's agriculture, industry and trade in the interests of the whole population.

SOCIAL REVOLUTIONARY PARTY. This party drew its main support from the peasants and at times co-operated with the Bolsheviks. It was suppressed after the 1917 Revolution.

SOVIET. Russian for 'council'. Workers' soviets were set up in factories, villages and towns during the 1905 Revolution. They later helped to pave the way for the 1917 Revolutions.

Soviets now form the organization of government. They range in importance from the small village soviet to the Supreme Soviet, which is the U.S.S.R.'s Parliament. At present only members of the Communist Party or its supporters are allowed to stand for election to the soviets.

The System of Soviets
Supreme Soviet of the U.S.S.R.
↓
Supreme Soviet of an Individual Republic (e.g. the Ukraine)
↓
Soviet of a Province
↓
Soviet of a District or City
↓
Soviet of a Village

SOVKHOZES. State farms owned and run by the government. In 1954 the Virgin Lands were opened up in an attempt to promote the expansion of agriculture. Half a million people settled in this vast area and, unlike the kolkhoz workers who earned money by selling produce, they were paid wages by the government. Mainly due to adverse climatic conditions the scheme was not a total success.

SPECIALIZED AGENCIES. Sections of the United Nations which aim to promote the welfare of the peoples of the world, especially those in poor countries, in particular fields; e.g. health (World Health Organization), food production (Food and Agricultural Organization).

SPUTNIK. On 4th October, 1957, the Russians launched Sputnik I ('Fellow Traveller'). It was the first artificial satellite to be put into orbit around the earth and marked the beginning of the 'space-race'.

WHITE ARMY. The 'Whites' was the collective name given to those Russians opposed to the Bolshevik cause. Small representative governments usually acted independently of one another and held to a wide range of political ideals. Their first, badly organised, army was led by General Denikin and after initial victories it eventually crumbled under attacks from the Red Army in 1922. 'White' armies were supported by Britain, France, America and Japan.

ZEMSTVA. Elected bodies, rather like county councils, which were set up in Russia in 1864 to deal with such matters as hospitals, roads and education. They lasted until 1917.

Further Reading

Secondary Level Books

Making the Modern World: Russia, John Robottom (Longman, 1972).
The Growth of Modern Russia, John Kennett (Blackie, 1967).
Lenin and the Downfall of Tsarist Russia, Elizabeth Roberts (Methuen, 1966).
Russia, John Lawrence (Methuen, 1965).
The U.S.S.R., G. M. Howe (Hulton, 1972).
The Russian Revolutions, David Footman (Faber & Faber, 1962).
Stalin, Man of Steel, Elizabeth Roberts (Methuen, 1968).
Twentieth Century Russia, Sally Pickering (O.U.P., 1965).
Soviet Russia, John Lawrence (Benn, 1967).
The Cold War, Paul Hastings (Benn, 1969).

More Advanced Books

Daily Life in Russia under the last Tsar, H. Troyat (Allen & Unwin, 1961).
A History of Russia, G. Vernadsky (Yale U.P., 1961).
Khruschev Remembers, ed. Edward Crankshaw (Deutsch, 1971).
Lenin, David Shub (Penguin Books, 1966).
The Making of Modern Russia, Lionel Kochan (Penguin Books, 1970).
Endurance and Endeavour: Russian History 1812-1971, J. N. Westwood (O.U.P. 1973).
Russia: A Short History, Michael Florinsky (Collier-Macmillan, 1969).
The Russian Revolution, Alan Moorehead (Panther, 1960).
The Soviet Achievement, J. Nett (Thames & Hudson, 1967).
Soviet Union in Maps, ed. Harold Fullard (Philip, 1972).
Stalin, Isaac Deutscher (Penguin Books, 1970).

Literature

And Quiet Flows the Don, M. Sholokhov (Penguin, 1967).
Dr. Zhivago, B. Pasternak (Fontana 1969).
One Day in the Life of Ivan Denisovich, A. Solzhenitsyn (Penguin, 1968).
In That Dawn, Konstantin Paustovsky (Harvill Press, 1964).

Index